See Mix Drink

See Mix Drink

A REFRESHINGLY SIMPLE GUIDE TO CRAFTING
THE WORLD'S MOST POPULAR COCKTAILS

Brian D. Murphy

LITTLE, BROWN AND COMPANY

New York | Boston | London

Little, Brown and Company
Hachette Book Group
237 Park Avenue, New York, NY 10017
www.hachettebookgroup.com

First Edition: October 2011

Little, Brown and Company is a division of Hachette Book
Group, Inc. The Little, Brown name and logo are trademarks
of Hachette Book Group, Inc.

The publisher is not responsible for websites (or their
content) that are not owned by the publisher.

ISBN 978-0-316-17671-2
LCCN 2011921792

10 9 8 7 6 5 4 3 2 1

SC

Graphic Design by Will Gunderson
Photography by Liz Banfield
Drink Styling by Nicole Murphy
Printed in China

Contents

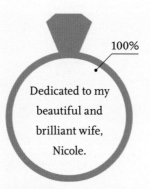

100%

Dedicated to my
beautiful and
brilliant wife,
Nicole.

Dear Friends,

It's time for a more intuitive cocktail-making book—one that adds unquestionable transparency to the mixing process. After being inspired to craft cocktails beyond the basics—Gin & Tonics and Rum & Colas—I became frustrated while trying to use conventional cocktail books. Like most people, I am a visual learner, yet most cocktail books on today's shelves are laden with text-based recipes and wordy instructions, utilizing the same claustrophobic formats that have remained unchanged for decades. For most, these books have become permanent fixtures on home bookshelves instead of becoming catalysts for cocktail-making adventure. It's time for a cocktail book revolution.

See Mix Drink empowers readers to become instant cocktail-making experts. This book brings intuitiveness and ease-of-use to cocktail making in an innovative visual format. Instead of featuring thousands of recipes for uncommon and unusual drinks, *See Mix Drink* focuses on the 100 most sought-after cocktails.

Creating this book was incredibly fun for me personally, as well as for my friends and family, who were able to test and refine the format (and try drinks!). I hope *See Mix Drink* becomes a useful and well-worn companion along your cocktail-making journey.

Cheers!
Brian D. Murphy

How to Use this Book

COCKTAIL PRONUNCIATION

Never mis-pruh-nouns cocktails again

Mint Julep

mint joo-lip

COCKTAIL "SNAPSHOT"

Demystifies cocktails by visually representing drink-ingredient volumes

KEY

Assigns colors to ingredients

INGREDIENTS

Quick reference guide for gathering the ingredients and barware/glassware necessary to begin mixing (see pages 10–13 for glassware, barware, and ingredient assumptions)

½ oz.

2 ½ oz.

INGREDIENTS

KEY

■ Whiskey (Bourbon)
▨ Simple Syrup
♣ Mint Leaves

NOTE

There are a number of ways to mix cocktails. However, the instructions included in this book are meant to be a starting point for more advanced mixology. Once you have mastered the techniques included in *See Mix Drink*, mixing any drink is possible.

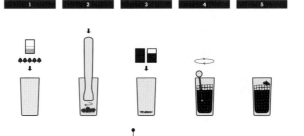

DESCRIPTION

Explains the origins of cocktails along with any ingredient variations or substitutions

BEST OCCASION

Highlighted icon denotes the traditional occasion for enjoying the cocktail

- Morning
- Before Dinner
- After Dinner
- Anytime

TIME REQUIRED

Indicates estimated time for preparation (including ingredient gathering and garnish cutting) and cocktail mixing

PROPORTIONS & CALORIES

Illustrates the liquid proportions in each drink. Calories per drink are included for the health conscious.

TEXT INSTRUCTIONS

Helpful supplement to the visual instructions below

VISUAL INSTRUCTIONS

Intuitive icons depict simple, yet very specific, visual instructions for mixing the cocktails. Note: use exact amounts and quantities shown (e.g., five mint leaves should be used for the Mint Julep).

199

DESCRIPTION

The Mint Julep is well known as the official cocktail of the Kentucky Derby. Each year, an estimated 120,000 Mint Juleps are served at the Churchill Downs horse track over the two-day Kentucky Oaks and Kentucky Derby races.

BEST OCCASION

TIME REQUIRED 3 MINUTES
Prep: 1 min   Mix: 2 min

PROPORTIONS

17%   83%
Calories 218

FINISHED DRINK

INSTRUCTIONS

1 Combine simple syrup and 5 mint leaves into a highball glass. 2 Muddle well. 3 Pour in whiskey. 4 Fill with crushed ice and stir. 5 Garnish with mint sprig.

1   2   3   4   5

Bar Essentials

Below is the glassware used throughout this book, along with the maximum volume of liquid each glass is capable of holding. The volumes chosen were based on average glass sizes commonly found in most homes.

COCKTAIL GLASS

8 oz.

Also known as a martini glass, the cocktail glass has become an icon synonymous with cocktails. The cocktail glass is the preferred container for drinks prepared without ice, or "straight up."

ROCKS GLASS

8 oz.

Also known as an old fashioned glass or lowball, the rocks glass is the preferred container for smaller volume drinks with ice, or "on the rocks."

HIGHBALL GLASS

10 oz.

The highball glass is most commonly used for high-volume drinks served "on the rocks," or with ice. It is used for many classic cocktails, including the Bloody Mary and Long Island Iced Tea.

CHAMPAGNE FLUTE

8 oz.

The Champagne flute was designed specifically for Champagne— uniquely shaped to prevent bubbles from escaping the glass.

MUG

10 oz.

Mugs are typically short, heavier glasses used to serve hot drinks, such as the Irish Coffee and the Hot Toddy. The handle remains cool while the mug and its contents are hot.

SHOT GLASS

1 ½ oz.

A shot glass is used to serve shots of liquor and as a measuring device for mixed drinks. Shot glasses range in size from ½ ounce to 2 ounces, with 1 ½ ounces being the most common.

Below are the barware and equipment used in the drink-mixing process.

SHAKER

Used when mixing ingredients by shaking with ice, often vigorously to ensure maximum blending.

STRAINER "HAWTHORNE STRAINER"

Used to strain the mixed contents from a cocktail shaker. The spring coils ensure a tight seal on shakers.

STIRRING SPOON

A stirring spoon mixes cocktail ingredients together without "bruising" the spirits. Some stirring spoons even work as a measuring device for teaspoon amounts.

MUDDLER

A specialized small wooden stick, a muddler is used to mash herbs, fruit, and peels to release flavors and blend them more easily with other ingredients.

BLENDER

Used to crush ice and ingredients. For frozen drinks.

The Spirits

BRANDY

Produced:	Made from wine or fermented fruit juice
Origin:	Holland, 16th century
Alcohol Content:	40% (80 proof)
Popular Brands:	Christian Brothers, E&J, Hennessy, Rémy Martin
Types/Variations:	*Cognac:* made from wine in Cognac, France *Armagnac:* produced from grapes grown in the Armagnac region of France *Fruit Brandy:* made from fermented fruit juice (e.g., apple, cherry, apricot)

CHAMPAGNE

Produced:	In-bottle secondary fermentation of wine; must be produced in the Champagne region of France to be called "Champagne"
Origin:	England, 17th century
Alcohol Content:	13% (26 proof)
Popular Brands:	Dom Pérignon, Korbel, Moët & Chandon
Types/Variations:	*Brut:* small amount of sweetening added to remove dryness *Demi-sec:* sweet *Sec:* medium-sweet *Extra Sec:* dry

GIN

Produced:	Made by re-distilling a neutral grain-based spirit with juniper berries and other botanicals
Origin:	Holland, 17th century
Alcohol Content:	40% (80 proof)
Popular Brands:	Beefeater, Bombay Sapphire, Hendrick's, Tanqueray
Types/Variations:	*London Dry Gin:* unsweetened (most popular type of gin) *Plymouth Gin:* slightly sweetened *Flavored Gin:* infused with various flavors (e.g., cucumber, lime, orange)

RUM

Produced:	Made by distilling sugar cane
Origin:	Caribbean, 17th century
Alcohol Content:	40% (80 proof)
Popular Brands:	Bacardi, Captain Morgan, Malibu, Mount Gay, Myers's
Types/Variations:	*Light Rum:* colorless; sweet flavor *Dark Rum:* dark brown in color; rich flavors include caramel and molasses *Flavored Rum:* various flavors added (e.g., coconut, pineapple, mango)

TEQUILA

Produced:	Made from the blue agave plant
Origin:	Mexico, 16th century
Alcohol Content:	40% (80 proof)
Popular Brands:	Cabo Wabo, Don Julio, Jose Cuervo, Patrón, Sauza
Types/Variations:	*Silver/White:* colorless; strong flavor; bottled immediately after distillation
	Reposado: meaning "rested"; aged between two months and one year in oak barrels before bottling
	Añejo: meaning "aged"; aged for at least one year

VODKA

Produced:	Made from fermented grain or potatoes
Origin:	Russia, 14th century
Alcohol Content:	40% (80 proof)
Popular Brands:	Absolut, Grey Goose, Ketel One, Stolichnaya
Types/Variations:	*Flavored Vodka:* various flavors added (e.g., lemon, lime, mint, orange, pepper, peach, strawberry)

WHISKEY

Produced:	Made from distilled grain
Origin:	Scotland, 15th century
Alcohol Content:	40% (80 proof)
Popular Brands:	Crown Royal, Jack Daniel's, Jameson, Jim Beam, Knob Creek, Maker's Mark
Types/Variations:	*Bourbon:* made in Kentucky; sweet in flavor
	Canadian: made in Canada; light and smooth flavor
	Irish: made in Ireland; aged for at least three years
	Rye: made mostly in the U.S.; distinctive spicy and fruity flavor
	Scotch: made in Scotland; aged for at least three years; smoky flavor

HOW TO MAKE SIMPLE SYRUP

Simple Syrup is simply sugar dissolved in water. The easiest and fastest way to make Simple Syrup is to combine equal parts sugar and water and then shake in a bottle or enclosed container.

12 oz.

Brandy

Between the Sheets

bih-tween thuh sheets

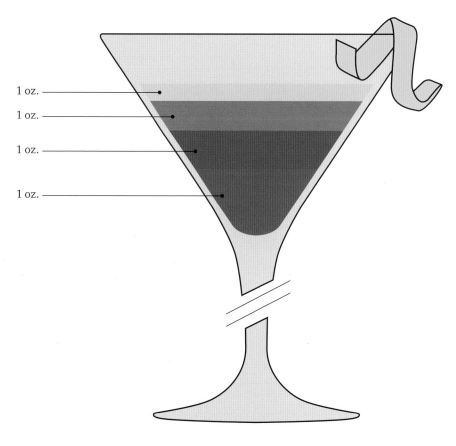

1 oz.
1 oz.
1 oz.

1 oz.

INGREDIENTS

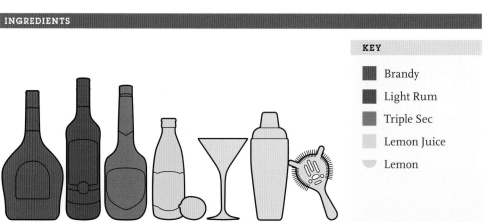

KEY

Brandy

Light Rum

Triple Sec

Lemon Juice

Lemon

DESCRIPTION

Between the Sheets is a strong cocktail that is said to have originated in Paris during the early 1930s. It is the variation of the Sidecar. Try substituting brandy with peach schnapps for a fruitier alternative.

BEST OCCASION

TIME REQUIRED   3 MINUTES

Prep: 2 min   Mix: 1 min

PROPORTIONS

25%   25%

Calories
249

25%   25%

FINISHED DRINK

INSTRUCTIONS

1 Combine brandy, light rum, triple sec, and lemon juice in a cocktail shaker. **2** Shake with ice. **3** Strain into a chilled cocktail glass. **4** Garnish with a lemon twist.

| 1 | 2 | 3 | 4 |

Brandy Alexander

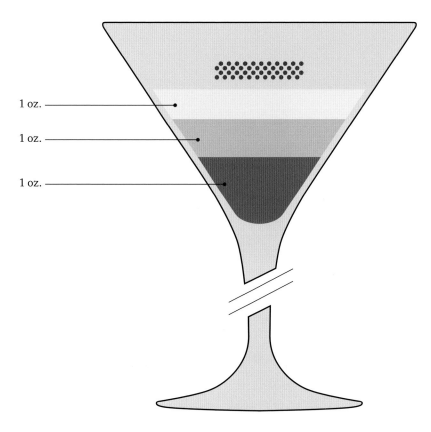

1 oz.

1 oz.

1 oz.

INGREDIENTS

KEY

- Brandy
- Dark Crème de Cacao
- Half-and-half
- Ground Nutmeg

DESCRIPTION

Created in the early twentieth century, the Brandy Alexander is considered to be one of the most sophisticated after-dinner drinks. The cocktail is smooth and creamy and pairs well with chocolate desserts.

BEST OCCASION

TIME REQUIRED — 2 MINUTES

| Prep: 1 min | Mix: 1 min |

PROPORTIONS

FINISHED DRINK

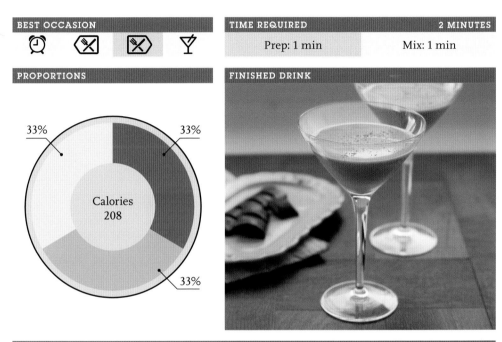

33%   33%

Calories
208

33%

INSTRUCTIONS

1 Combine brandy, dark crème de cacao, and half-and-half in a cocktail shaker. **2** Shake with ice. **3** Strain into a chilled cocktail glass. **4** Garnish with a sprinkling of nutmeg.

| 1 | 2 | 3 | 4 |

Brandy Daisy

bran-dee dey-zee

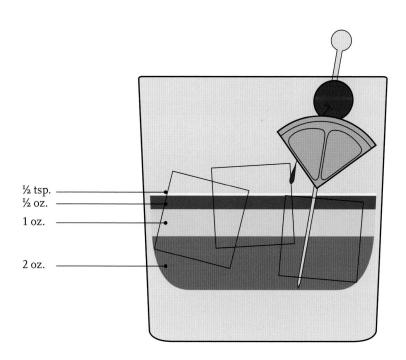

½ tsp.
½ oz.
1 oz.
2 oz.

INGREDIENTS

KEY

Brandy
Lemon Juice
Grenadine
Superfine Sugar
Orange
Cherry

DESCRIPTION

Along with the Sidecar, the Brandy Daisy was a popular drink in the late nineteenth century and early twentieth century, particularly during World War I. Try substituting brandy with rum.

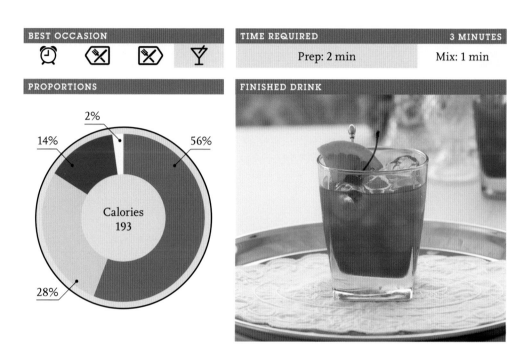

BEST OCCASION

TIME REQUIRED   3 MINUTES

Prep: 2 min   Mix: 1 min

PROPORTIONS

2%
14%
56%
Calories
193
28%

FINISHED DRINK

INSTRUCTIONS

1 Combine brandy, lemon juice, grenadine, and superfine sugar in a cocktail shaker.
2 Shake with ice. **3** Pour the contents into a rocks glass with ice. **4** Garnish with an orange wedge and cherry.

| 1 | 2 | 3 | 4 |

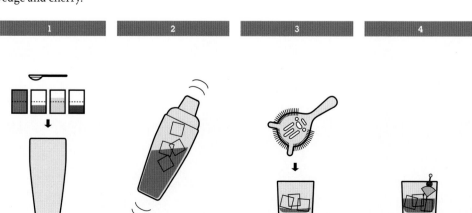

Corpse Reviver

kawrps ri-vahyv-er

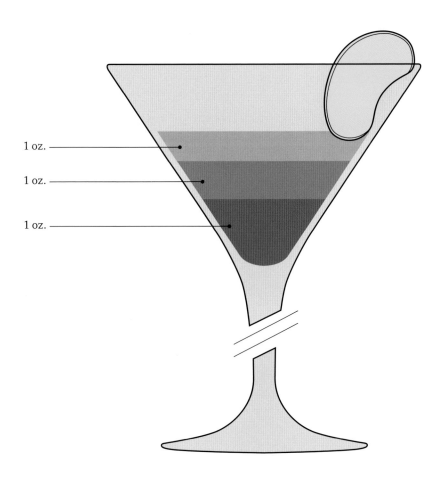

1 oz.

1 oz.

1 oz.

INGREDIENTS

KEY

- Brandy
- Apple Brandy
- Sweet Vermouth
- Green Apple

DESCRIPTION

While a few variations of the Corpse Reviver exist, according to several drink historians, the original was created by Frank Meier at the Ritz Bar in Paris, France. The Corpse Reviver is taken "before 11 a.m. or whenever steam and energy are needed," according to Henry Craddock in *The Savoy Cocktail Book*. This drink is particularly popular at Halloween parties in the U.S.

BEST OCCASION

TIME REQUIRED   **3 MINUTES**

Prep: 2 min	Mix: 1 min

PROPORTIONS

FINISHED DRINK

33%   33%

Calories
178

33%

INSTRUCTIONS

1 Combine brandy, apple brandy, and sweet vermouth in a cocktail shaker. **2** Shake with ice. **3** Strain into a chilled cocktail glass. **4** Garnish with an apple slice.

1	2	3	4

Eggnog

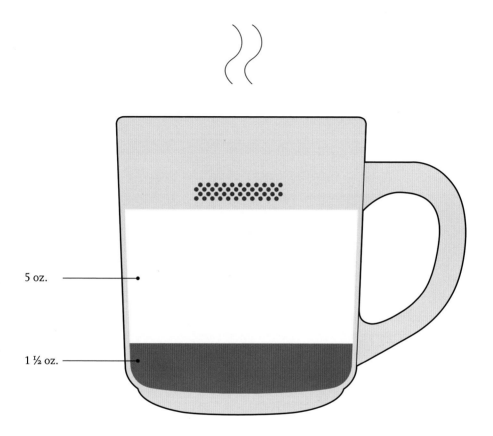

5 oz.

1 ½ oz.

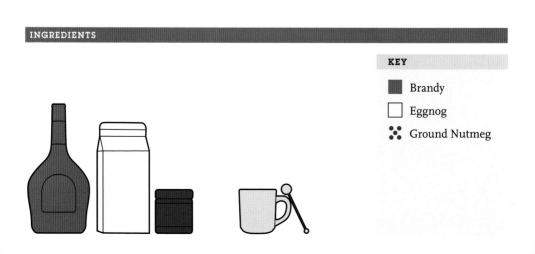

KEY

- Brandy
- Eggnog
- Ground Nutmeg

DESCRIPTION

A staple for winter holiday gatherings and parties, Eggnog is a smooth and sweet delight, pairing well with cookies or other treats. Try substituting brandy with whiskey for a slightly edgier taste.

BEST OCCASION

TIME REQUIRED   2 MINUTES

Prep: 1 min	Mix: 1 min

PROPORTIONS

FINISHED DRINK

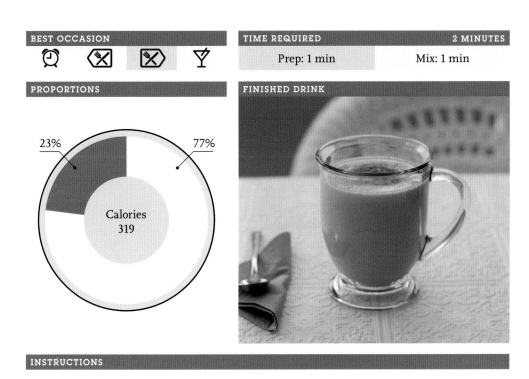

23%   77%

Calories
319

INSTRUCTIONS

1 Pour brandy and eggnog into a mug. **2** Stir well. **3** Garnish with a sprinkling of nutmeg.

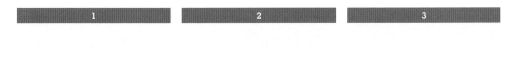

1	2	3

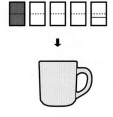

Horse's Neck

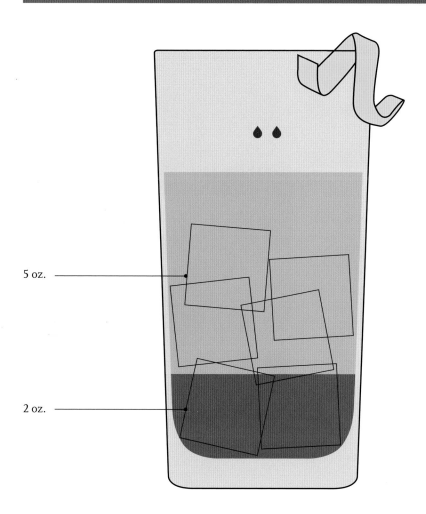

5 oz.

2 oz.

INGREDIENTS

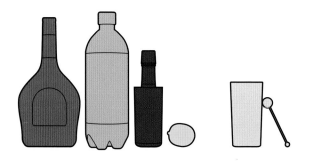

KEY

- Brandy
- Ginger Ale
- Bitters
- Lemon

DESCRIPTION

While the original recipe was without alcohol, in the early 1920s brandy was added to make the Horse's Neck a truly refreshing cocktail. The lemon peel is used to resemble the neck of a horse dipping its head into the drink.

BEST OCCASION

TIME REQUIRED   3 MINUTES

Prep: 2 min	Mix: 1 min

PROPORTIONS

FINISHED DRINK

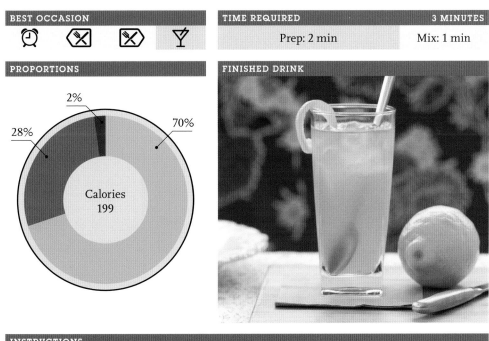

2%
28%
70%

Calories
199

INSTRUCTIONS

1 Pour brandy, ginger ale, and bitters (2 dashes) into a highball glass with ice. **2** Stir well.
3 Garnish with a lemon twist.

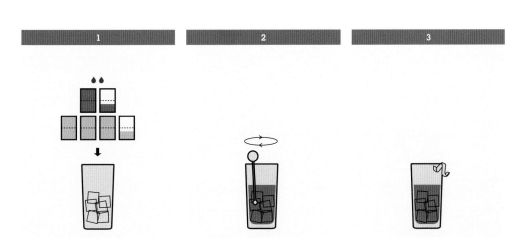

Jack Rose

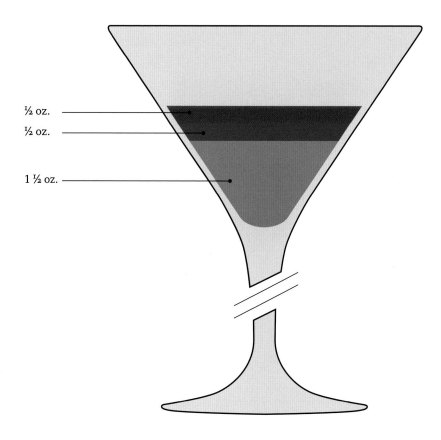

½ oz.

½ oz.

1 ½ oz.

INGREDIENTS

KEY

Apple Brandy

Grenadine

Lime Juice

DESCRIPTION

While there are a number of possible origins behind the Jack Rose, many claim the drink gets its name from the combination of "applejack" (another name for apple brandy) and the "rose" color of the drink caused by the addition of grenadine.

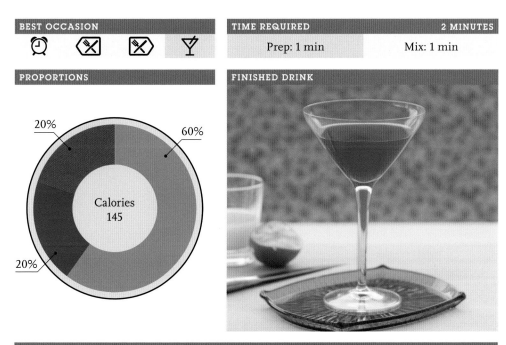

BEST OCCASION

TIME REQUIRED   2 MINUTES

Prep: 1 min   Mix: 1 min

PROPORTIONS

20%
60%
20%
Calories
145

FINISHED DRINK

INSTRUCTIONS

1 Combine apple brandy, grenadine, and lime juice in a cocktail shaker. **2** Shake with ice.
3 Strain into a chilled cocktail glass.

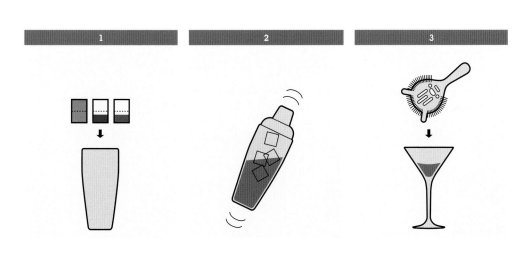

Metropolitan

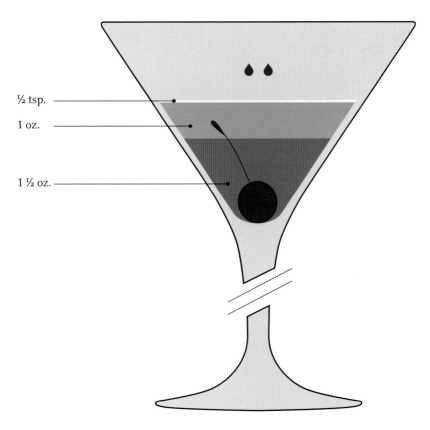

½ tsp.

1 oz.

1 ½ oz.

INGREDIENTS

KEY

- ▮ Brandy
- ▮ Sweet Vermouth
- ▯ Superfine Sugar
- ◆ Angostura Bitters
- ● Cherry

DESCRIPTION

A different take on the Cosmopolitan, the Metropolitan was created in the early 1990s in New York City.

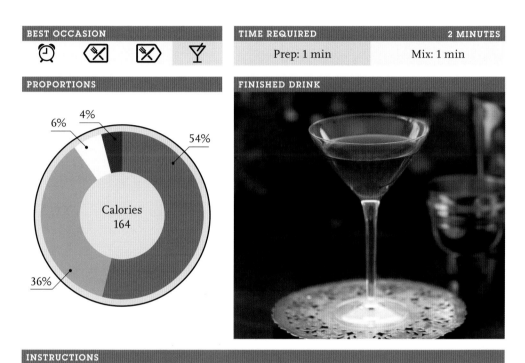

BEST OCCASION

TIME REQUIRED   2 MINUTES

Prep: 1 min	Mix: 1 min

PROPORTIONS

4%
6%
54%
Calories
164
36%

FINISHED DRINK

INSTRUCTIONS

1 Combine brandy, sweet vermouth, superfine sugar, and Angostura bitters (2 dashes) in a cocktail shaker. **2** Shake with ice. **3** Strain into a chilled cocktail glass. **4** Garnish with a cherry.

1	2	3	4

Sidecar

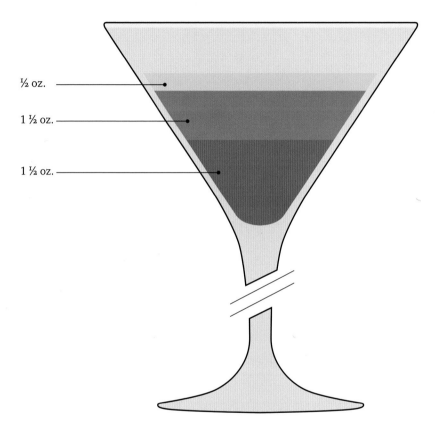

½ oz.

1 ½ oz.

1 ½ oz.

INGREDIENTS

KEY

- Brandy
- Triple Sec
- Lemon Juice
- Sugar

DESCRIPTION

The Sidecar is a classic cocktail that some claim was invented at the Ritz Hotel in Paris, France, during World War I. According to drink historians, a captain staying at the Ritz was often driven to the hotel in the sidecar of a motorcycle. He would arrive cold after being in the sidecar at night, so he requested a pre-dinner drink that would warm him up—a drink that became known as the Sidecar.

BEST OCCASION

TIME REQUIRED   3 MINUTES

Prep: 1 min   Mix: 2 min

PROPORTIONS

14%   43%

Calories
176

43%

FINISHED DRINK

INSTRUCTIONS

1 Apply sugar to a wet cocktail glass rim. **2** Combine brandy, triple sec, and lemon juice in a cocktail shaker. **3** Shake with ice. **4** Strain into a chilled cocktail glass.

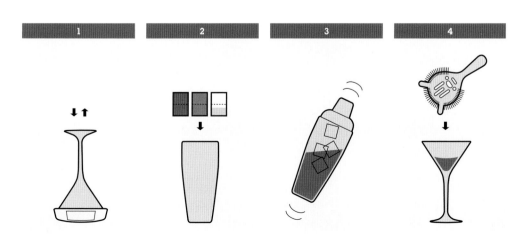

| 1 | 2 | 3 | 4 |

Champagne

Bellini

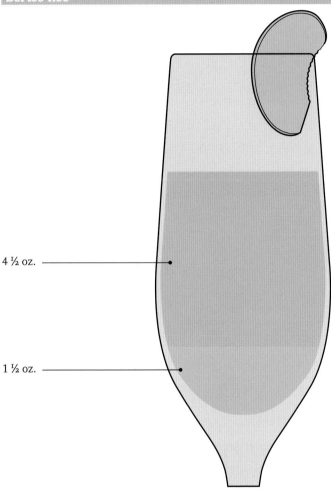

4 ½ oz.

1 ½ oz.

Champagne

White Peach Puree

 Peach

The Bellini was created by Giuseppe Cipriani at Harry's Bar in Venice, Italy, in 1948. Due to the cocktail's pink hue, Cipriani named the drink after the fifteenth-century Venetian artist Giovanni Bellini, who was known for using vivid pink colors in his paintings. Try substituting peach puree with one ounce of peach schnapps.

BEST OCCASION

TIME REQUIRED — 2 ½ MINUTES

Prep: 2 min | Mix: 30 sec

PROPORTIONS

FINISHED DRINK

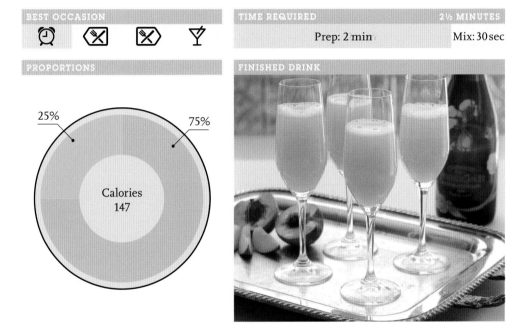

25%   75%

Calories
147

INSTRUCTIONS

1 Quarter-fill a Champagne flute with white peach puree. 2 Top with Champagne. 3 Garnish with a peach wedge (optional).

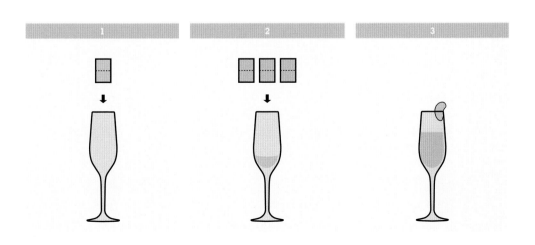

Black Velvet

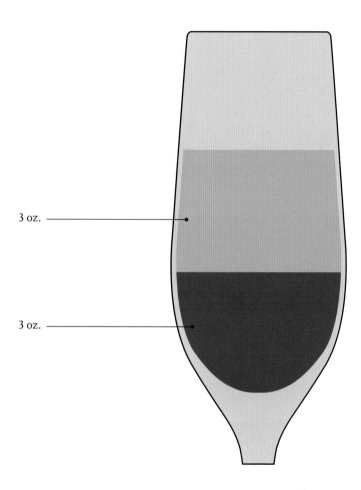

3 oz.

3 oz.

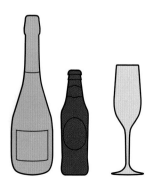

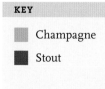

Champagne

Stout

DESCRIPTION

Believed to have been created by a bartender at Brooks Club in London, England, in 1891, the Black Velvet was born while the country was in mourning after Queen Victoria's husband, Prince Albert, died. The bartender thought Champagne was too celebratory for the occasion, so he combined it with stout. A Velvet is made with porter instead of stout.

BEST OCCASION				TIME REQUIRED	1½ MINUTES
				Prep: 1 min	Mix: 30 sec

PROPORTIONS

FINISHED DRINK

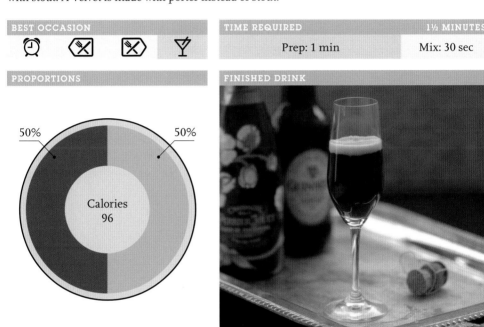

50%   50%

Calories
96

INSTRUCTIONS

1 Fill a Champagne flute halfway with stout (e.g., Guinness). 2 Top with Champagne.

Champagne Cocktail

sham-peyn kok-teyl

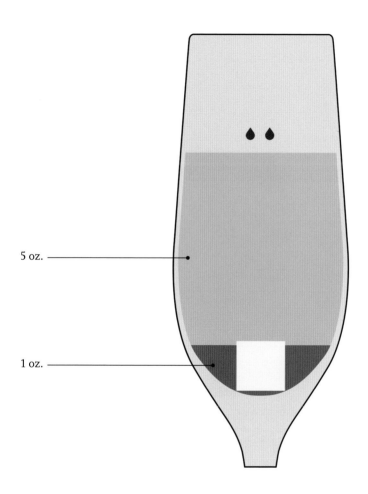

5 oz. —————

1 oz. —————

KEY

Champagne

Brandy

Angostura Bitters

Sugar Cube

DESCRIPTION

This drink takes its roots from a New York cocktail competition in 1889. The gold medal was awarded to bartender John Doughty based on a drink he called "Business Brace." This drink is said to be the predecessor of the Champagne Cocktail.

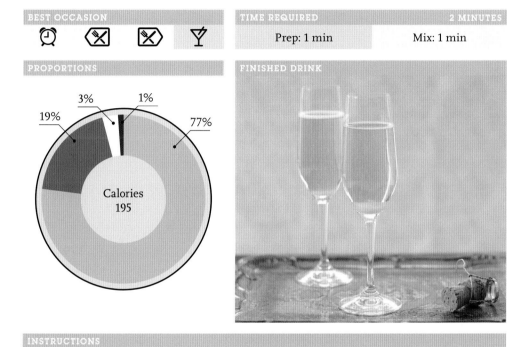

BEST OCCASION

TIME REQUIRED — 2 MINUTES

Prep: 1 min   Mix: 1 min

PROPORTIONS

3%   1%
19%   77%

Calories
195

FINISHED DRINK

INSTRUCTIONS

1 Place a sugar cube in a Champagne flute. 2 Soak the sugar cube with brandy and Angostura bitters (2 dashes). 3 Top with Champagne.

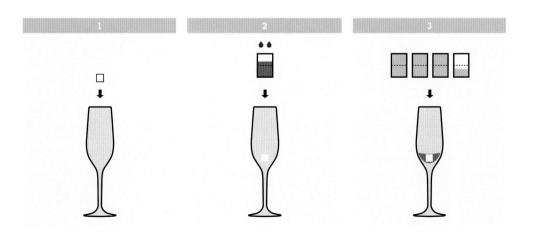

Kir Royale

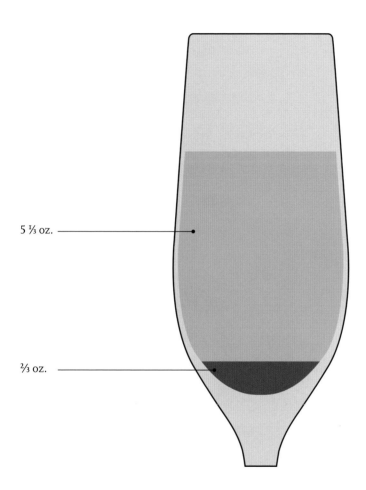

5 ⅓ oz. ————————

⅔ oz. ————————

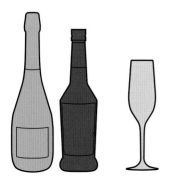

Champagne

Crème de Cassis

DESCRIPTION

After World War II, Felix Kir, the mayor of Dijon in Burgundy, France, wanted to promote his region's products, including wine, sparkling wine, and crème de cassis. While wine and crème de cassis make Kir, by replacing wine with Champagne, one creates the popular Kir Royale.

BEST OCCASION

TIME REQUIRED — 1½ MINUTES

Prep: 1 min	Mix: 30 sec

PROPORTIONS

FINISHED DRINK

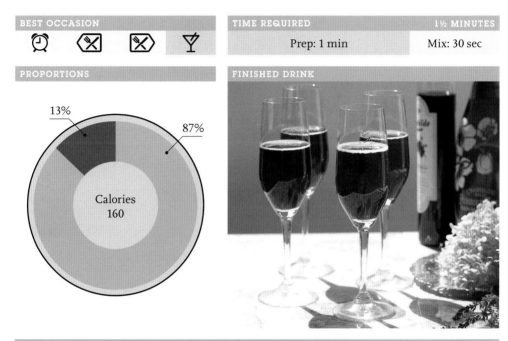

13%

87%

Calories
160

INSTRUCTIONS

1 Pour crème de cassis into a Champagne flute. 2 Top with Champagne.

1	2

Mimosa

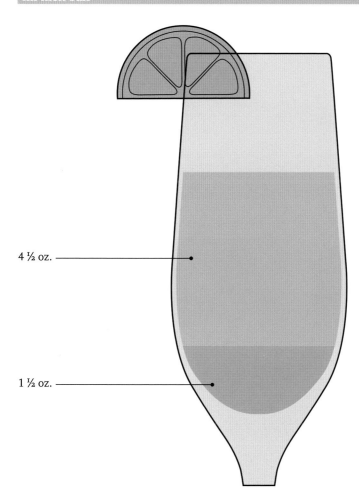

4 ½ oz. ———

1 ½ oz. ———

KEY

Champagne
Orange Juice
Orange

Named after the tropical Mimosa shrub, the Mimosa cocktail was created at the Ritz Hotel in Paris, France, in the mid-1920s and has remained a popular breakfast and wedding drink since.

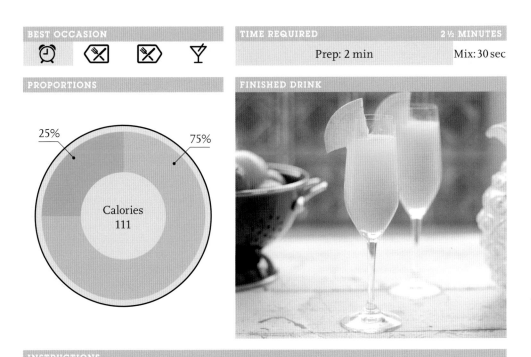

BEST OCCASION

TIME REQUIRED — 2 ½ MINUTES

Prep: 2 min   Mix: 30 sec

PROPORTIONS

25%   75%

Calories
111

FINISHED DRINK

INSTRUCTIONS

1 Quarter-fill a Champagne flute with orange juice. 2 Top with Champagne. 3 Garnish with an orange wedge.

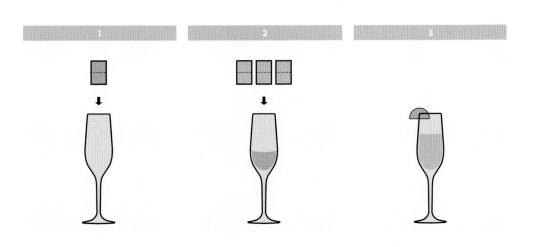

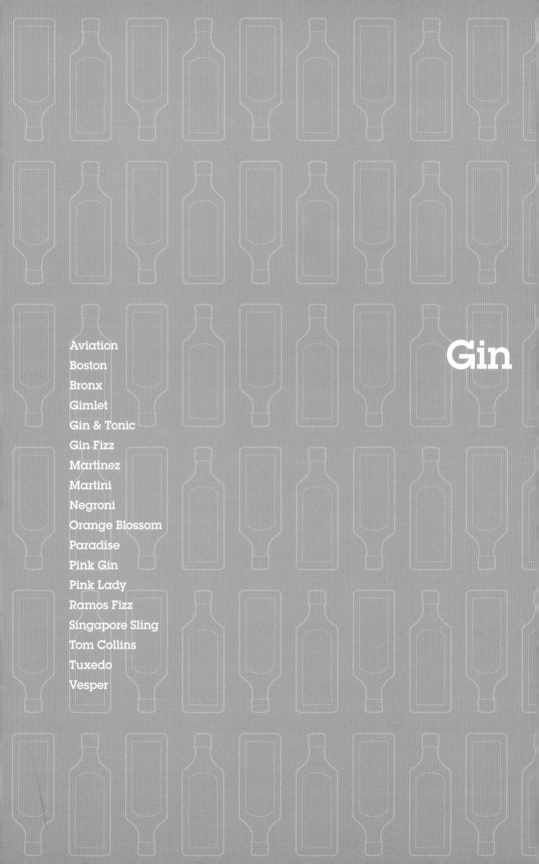

Gin

Aviation

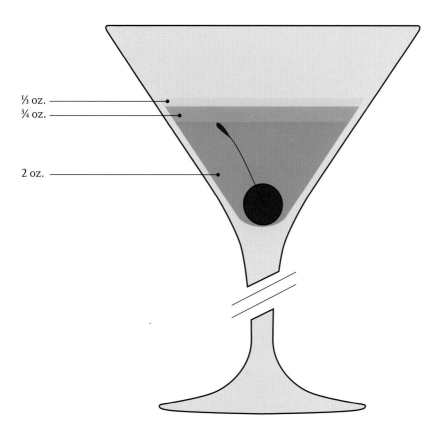

⅓ oz.
¾ oz.
2 oz.

INGREDIENTS

DESCRIPTION

While the origin of the Aviation remains a mystery, many agree the recipe was first printed in a 1916 book entitled *Recipes for Mixed Drinks* by Hugo Ensslin, the head bartender at Hotel Wallick in New York. An antidote to today's hectic airports and dizzying check-ins, the Aviation harkens back to a simpler and more elegant era, when flight was considered a relaxing luxury.

BEST OCCASION

TIME REQUIRED — **2 MINUTES**

Prep: 1 min	Mix: 1 min

PROPORTIONS

FINISHED DRINK

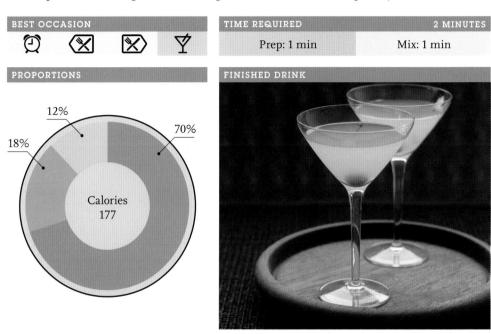

12%
18%
70%

Calories
177

INSTRUCTIONS

1 Combine gin, maraschino liqueur, and lemon juice in a cocktail shaker. **2** Shake with ice. **3** Strain into a chilled cocktail glass. **4** Garnish with a cherry.

1	2	3	4

Boston

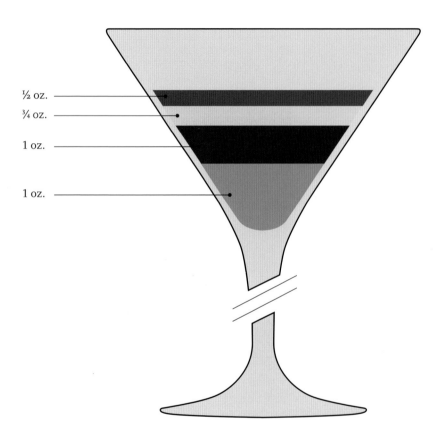

½ oz.

¾ oz.

1 oz.

1 oz.

INGREDIENTS

KEY

- Gin
- Apricot Brandy
- Lemon Juice
- Grenadine

DESCRIPTION

The Boston creatively combines gin with apricot brandy, making the drink surprisingly smooth, while the addition of fresh lemon juice adds a nice edge to the sweetness of the grenadine.

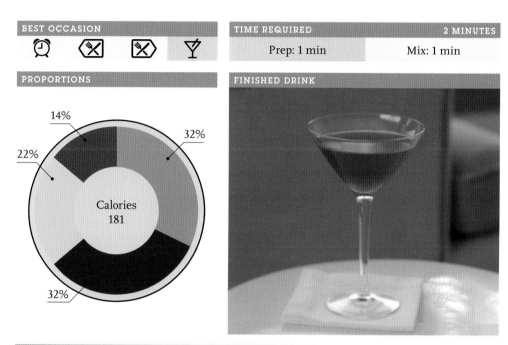

BEST OCCASION

TIME REQUIRED — **2 MINUTES**

Prep: 1 min | Mix: 1 min

PROPORTIONS

14%
32%
22%
Calories
181
32%

FINISHED DRINK

INSTRUCTIONS

1 Combine gin, apricot brandy, lemon juice, and grenadine in a cocktail shaker. 2 Shake with ice. 3 Strain into a chilled cocktail glass.

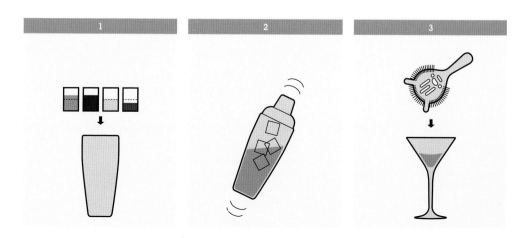

Bronx

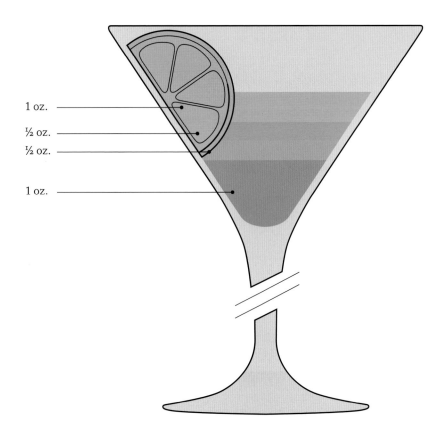

1 oz. —

½ oz. —

½ oz. —

1 oz. —

INGREDIENTS

KEY

- Gin
- Dry Vermouth
- Sweet Vermouth
- Orange Juice
- Orange

DESCRIPTION

One story has it that Johnnie Solon, a famous bartender at the Waldorf-Astoria, was inspired to create the Bronx in 1906 after visiting the newly opened Bronx Zoo. Others believe that the drink was invented in Philadelphia and later discovered by Bronx restaurateur Joseph Sormani in 1905. Whatever the case, the Bronx is a refreshing alternative to the Martini and Manhattan before dinner.

BEST OCCASION

TIME REQUIRED   **3 MINUTES**

| Prep: 2 min | Mix: 1 min |

PROPORTIONS

FINISHED DRINK

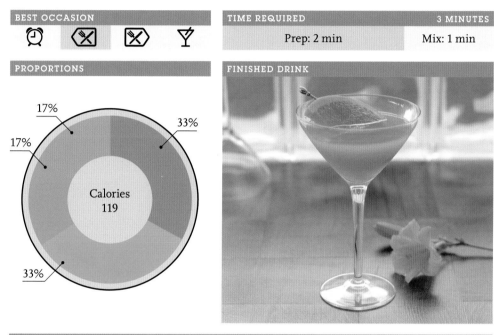

17%

33%

17%

Calories
119

33%

INSTRUCTIONS

1 Combine gin, dry vermouth, sweet vermouth, and orange juice in a cocktail shaker. 2 Shake with ice. 3 Strain into a chilled cocktail glass. 4 Garnish with an orange wedge.

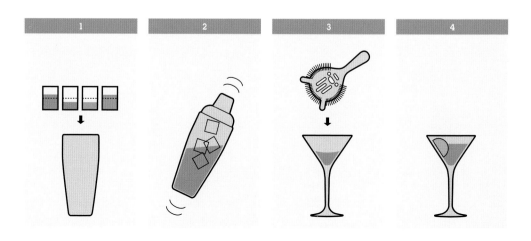

Gimlet

⅔ oz.

2 oz.

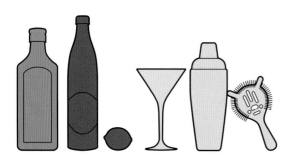

KEY

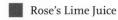

Gin

Rose's Lime Juice

 Lime

DESCRIPTION

The Gimlet is likely to have originated in the British Navy in the late nineteenth century. Lauchlin Rose, owner of a shipyard in Scotland, created a process for preserving lime juice during long voyages and labeled his product "Rose's Lime Cordial." Inevitably, naval officers began to mix their lime cordial with gin to make Gimlets. Try substituting gin with vodka for a Vodka Gimlet.

BEST OCCASION

TIME REQUIRED   3 MINUTES

Prep: 2 min   Mix: 1 min

PROPORTIONS

FINISHED DRINK

25%

75%

Calories
165

INSTRUCTIONS

1 Combine gin and Rose's lime juice in a cocktail shaker. 2 Shake with ice. 3 Strain into a chilled cocktail glass. 4 Garnish with a lime wedge.

| 1 | 2 | 3 | 4 |

Gin & Tonic

jin aynd ton-ik

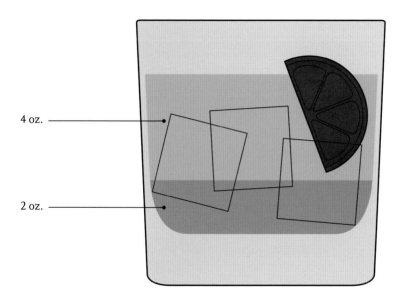

4 oz.

2 oz.

Gin

Tonic

Lime

DESCRIPTION

The Gin & Tonic is a classic summertime drink. The cocktail is said to have originated in India during the late nineteenth century, when some people believed gin would help ward off malaria, which tonic alone was traditionally used for. Try substituting gin with vodka to make a Vodka Tonic.

BEST OCCASION

TIME REQUIRED — **3 MINUTES**

Prep: 2 min	Mix: 1 min

PROPORTIONS

FINISHED DRINK

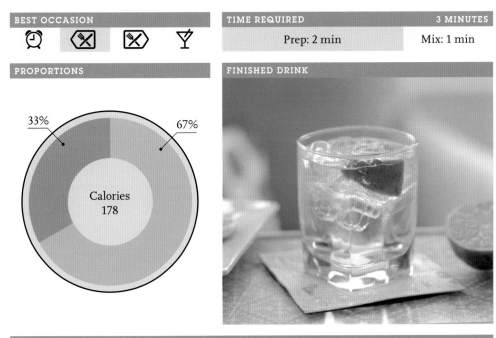

33%   67%

Calories
178

INSTRUCTIONS

1 Pour gin and tonic into a rocks glass with ice cubes. **2** Garnish with a lime wedge.

1	2

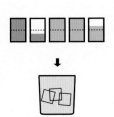

Gin Fizz

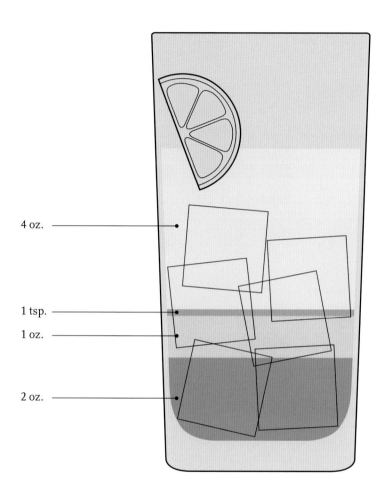

4 oz.

1 tsp.

1 oz.

2 oz.

INGREDIENTS

- Gin
- Lemon Juice
- Simple Syrup
- Club Soda
- Lemon

DESCRIPTION

The Gin Fizz was created in the nineteenth century and is considered a "sour" cocktail with soda water added. The addition of egg white creates a Silver Fizz, and when shaken with egg yolk, it becomes a Golden Fizz. A whole egg mixed with the Gin Fizz creates a Royal Fizz.

BEST OCCASION

TIME REQUIRED — 3 MINUTES

Prep: 2 min | Mix: 1 min

PROPORTIONS

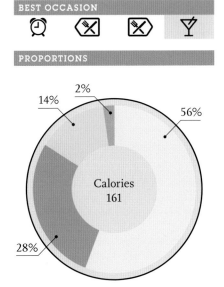

2%
14%
56%
Calories
161
28%

FINISHED DRINK

INSTRUCTIONS

1 Combine gin, lemon juice, and simple syrup in a cocktail shaker. **2** Shake with ice. **3** Strain into a highball glass filled with ice. **4** Pour in the club soda. **5** Garnish with a lemon wedge.

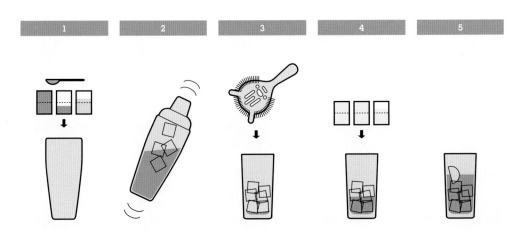

1 | 2 | 3 | 4 | 5

Martinez

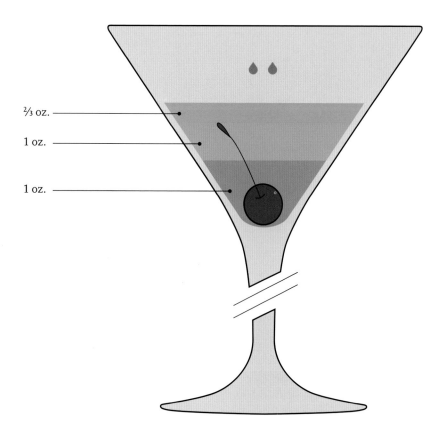

⅔ oz.

1 oz.

1 oz.

INGREDIENTS

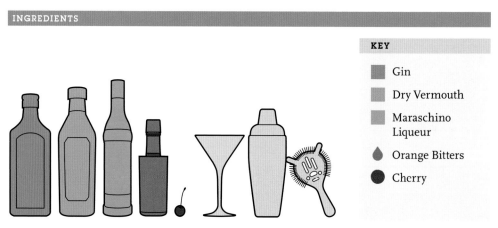

KEY

- Gin
- Dry Vermouth
- Maraschino Liqueur
- Orange Bitters
- Cherry

Believed to precede the Martini, the Martinez first appeared as a variation to the Manhattan in O.H. Byron's *The Modern Bartender* in 1884. Originally, the Martinez called for sweet vermouth instead of dry vermouth, giving it an amber color.

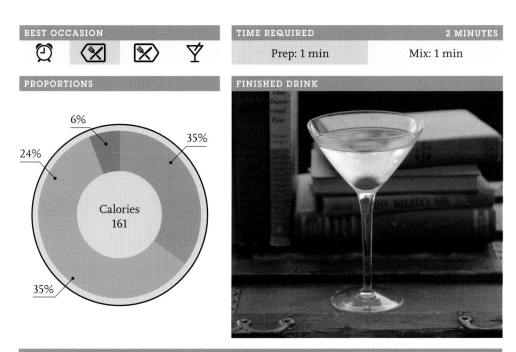

BEST OCCASION

TIME REQUIRED   **2 MINUTES**

Prep: 1 min   Mix: 1 min

PROPORTIONS

6%
35%
24%
Calories
161
35%

FINISHED DRINK

INSTRUCTIONS

1 Combine gin, dry vermouth, maraschino liqueur, and orange bitters (2 dashes) in a cocktail shaker. **2** Shake with ice. **3** Strain into a chilled cocktail glass. **4** Garnish with a cherry.

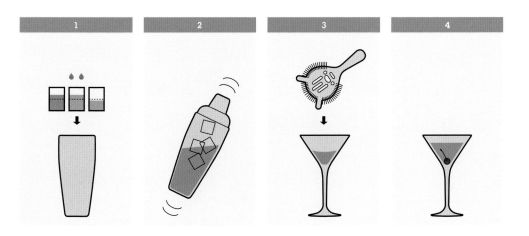

Martini

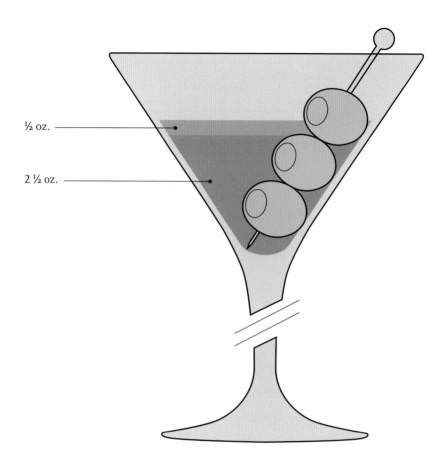

½ oz.

2 ½ oz.

INGREDIENTS

KEY

- Gin
- Dry Vermouth
- Green Olives

DESCRIPTION

The origin of the Martini is unclear, but there are a few stories, including that it was invented by an Italian vermouth distillery in the nineteenth century, by a bar in New York City in the early twentieth century, or as an adaptation of the Martinez. The addition of olive juice makes a Dirty Martini, while a Dry Martini includes very little or no dry vermouth.

BEST OCCASION

TIME REQUIRED — 2 MINUTES

Prep: 1 min   Mix: 1 min

PROPORTIONS

17%

83%

Calories
189

FINISHED DRINK

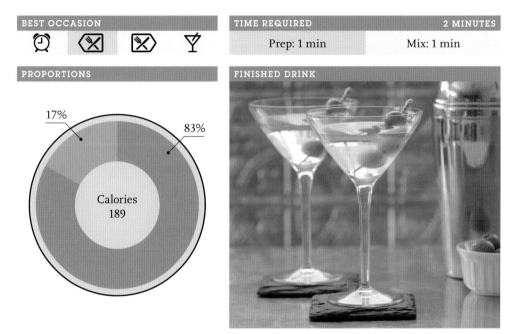

INSTRUCTIONS

1 Combine gin and dry vermouth in a cocktail shaker. **2** Shake with ice. **3** Strain into a chilled cocktail glass. **4** Garnish with green olives.

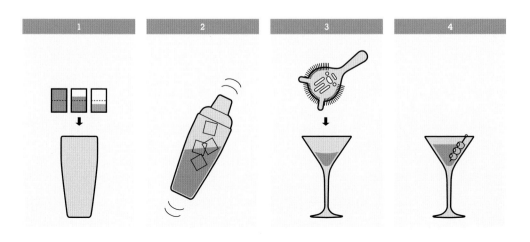

Negroni

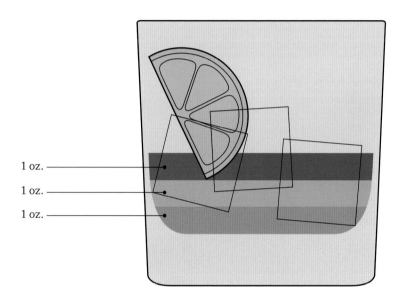

1 oz.
1 oz.
1 oz.

INGREDIENTS

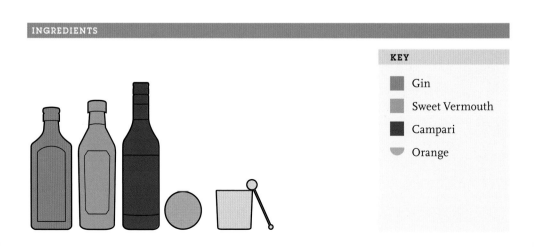

KEY

Gin

Sweet Vermouth

Campari

Orange

DESCRIPTION

According to cocktail lore, the Negroni was born in the 1920s when Count Camillo Negroni ordered an Americano (Campari and sweet vermouth) with gin while drinking at the Café Casoni in Florence, Italy. The Negroni is considered an acquired taste—people either love or hate the distinctive bitter and dry taste of the cocktail.

BEST OCCASION

TIME REQUIRED — 2 ½ MINUTES

Prep: 2 min | Mix: 30 sec

PROPORTIONS

FINISHED DRINK

33% 33% 33%

Calories 189

INSTRUCTIONS

1 Pour gin, sweet vermouth, and Campari into a rocks glass with ice cubes. 2 Stir well.
3 Garnish with an orange wedge.

1 | 2 | 3

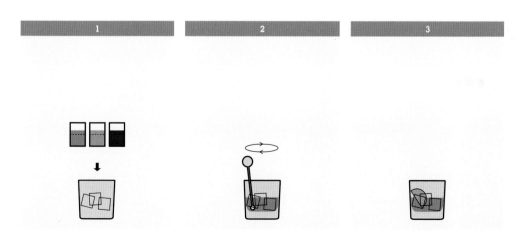

Orange Blossom

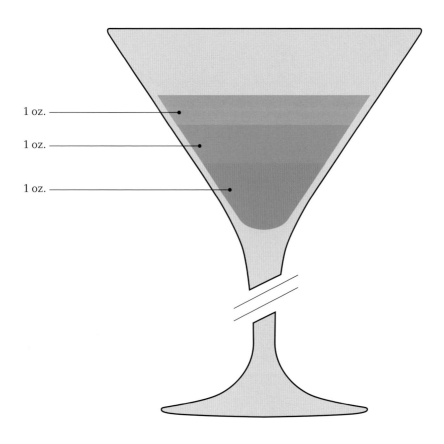

1 oz.

1 oz.

1 oz.

INGREDIENTS

KEY

- Gin
- Sweet Vermouth
- Orange Juice

DESCRIPTION

The Orange Blossom was created during the Prohibition years and was sometimes referred to as an Adirondack. The orange juice was presumably used to disguise the smell of gin.

BEST OCCASION

TIME REQUIRED — 2 MINUTES

Prep: 1 min   Mix: 1 min

PROPORTIONS

FINISHED DRINK

33%   33%

Calories
123

33%

INSTRUCTIONS

1 Combine gin, sweet vermouth, and orange juice in a cocktail shaker. 2 Shake with ice.
3 Strain into a chilled cocktail glass.

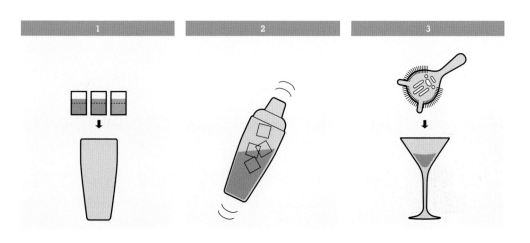

Paradise

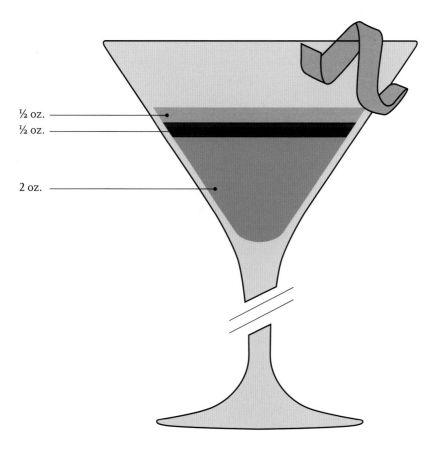

½ oz.
½ oz.

2 oz.

INGREDIENTS

KEY

- Gin
- Apricot Brandy
- Orange Juice
- Orange

DESCRIPTION

The Paradise is a pleasantly sweet and fruity alternative to the traditionally dry Martini as a pre-dinner drink. The origin of the Paradise is unknown.

BEST OCCASION

TIME REQUIRED   3 MINUTES

| Prep: 2 min | Mix: 1 min |

PROPORTIONS

FINISHED DRINK

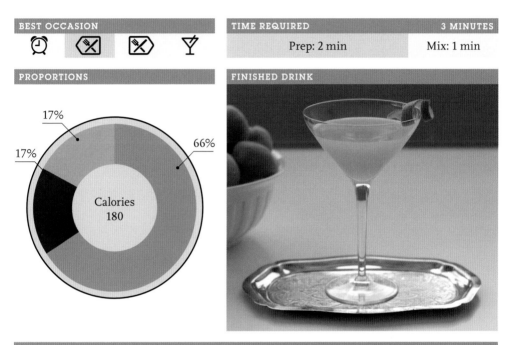

17%
17%
66%

Calories
180

INSTRUCTIONS

1 Combine gin, apricot brandy, and orange juice in a cocktail shaker. **2** Shake with ice.
3 Strain into a chilled cocktail glass. **4** Garnish with an orange twist.

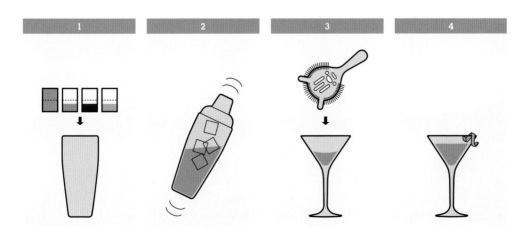

| 1 | 2 | 3 | 4 |

Pink Gin

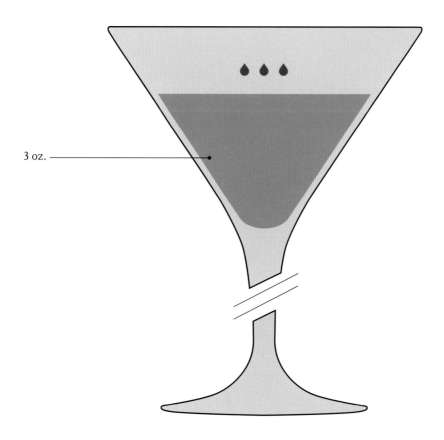

3 oz.

INGREDIENTS

■ Gin

 Angostura Bitters

DESCRIPTION

As with several gin drinks, the Pink Gin originated with the British Navy. Angostura bitters were found to calm sailors' upset stomachs, so the Navy added it to sailors' medicine kits and gin rations. The sailors quickly combined the bitters and gin to create the Pink Gin.

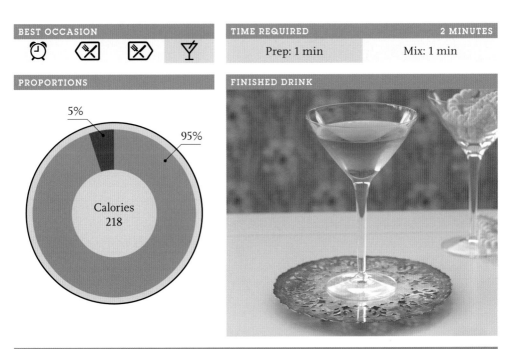

BEST OCCASION

TIME REQUIRED — 2 MINUTES

Prep: 1 min | Mix: 1 min

PROPORTIONS

5%
95%

Calories
218

FINISHED DRINK

INSTRUCTIONS

1 Combine gin and Angostura bitters (3 dashes) in a cocktail shaker. 2 Shake with ice.
3 Strain into a chilled cocktail glass.

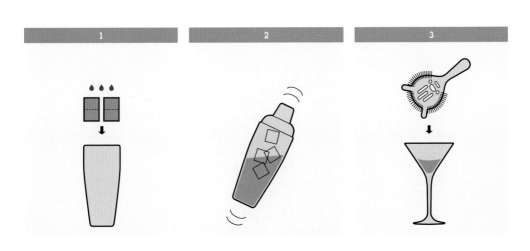

1 | 2 | 3

Pink Lady

pingk ley-dee

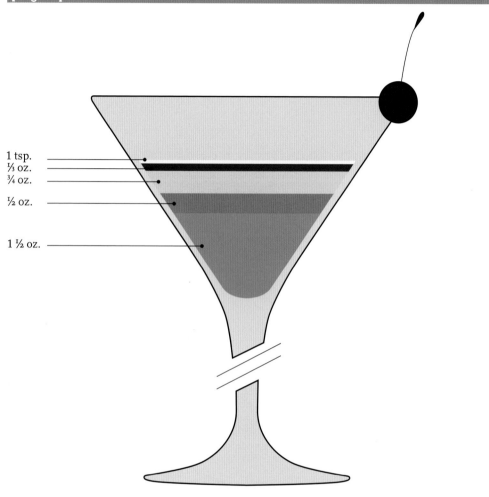

1 tsp.
⅓ oz.
¾ oz.

½ oz.

1 ½ oz.

INGREDIENTS

KEY

Gin

Apple Brandy

Lemon Juice

Grenadine

Egg-White Powder

Cherry

DESCRIPTION

The Pink Lady was named after a successful 1912 stage play and was a favorite among high-society women in the 1930s. Substitute grenadine with triple sec to create a White Lady.

BEST OCCASION

TIME REQUIRED   2 MINUTES

Prep: 1 min   Mix: 1 min

PROPORTIONS

5%
10%
16%
46%
23%

Calories
186

FINISHED DRINK

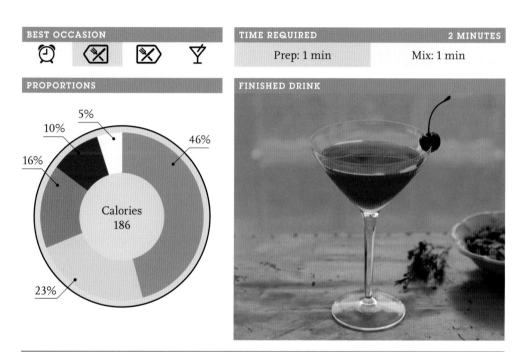

INSTRUCTIONS

1 Combine gin, apple brandy, lemon juice, grenadine, and egg-white powder in a cocktail shaker.
2 Shake with ice. 3 Strain into a chilled cocktail glass. 4 Garnish with a cherry.

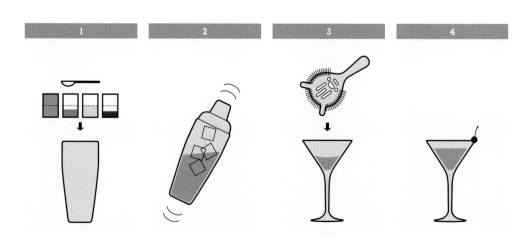

Ramos Fizz

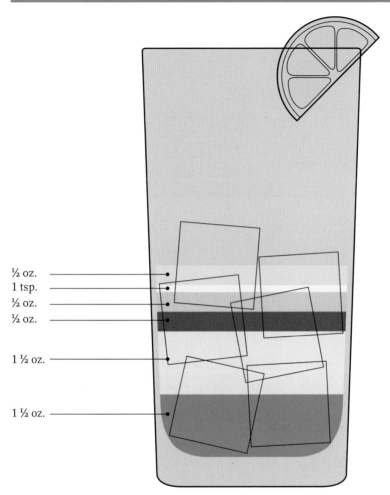

½ oz.
1 tsp.
½ oz.
½ oz.

1 ½ oz.

1 ½ oz.

INGREDIENTS

KEY

- Gin
- Half-and-Half
- Lime Juice
- Lemon Juice
- Egg-White Powder
- Club Soda
- Lemon

DESCRIPTION

The Ramos Fizz was created by Henrico Ramos, who owned the Imperial Cabinet Saloon in New Orleans. The recipe was kept a secret until the saloon closed during Prohibition, when Henrico's brother published the recipe in a full-page advertisement.

BEST OCCASION

TIME REQUIRED   3 MINUTES

Prep: 2 min	Mix: 1 min

PROPORTIONS

FINISHED DRINK

Calories 187

3%
11%
11%
32%
11%
32%

INSTRUCTIONS

1 Combine gin, half-and-half, lemon juice, lime juice, and egg-white powder in a cocktail shaker.
2 Shake with ice. **3** Strain into a highball glass filled with ice. **4** Pour in the club soda.
5 Garnish with a lemon wedge.

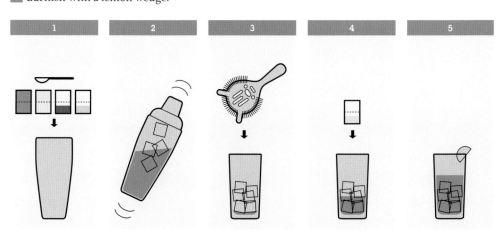

Singapore Sling

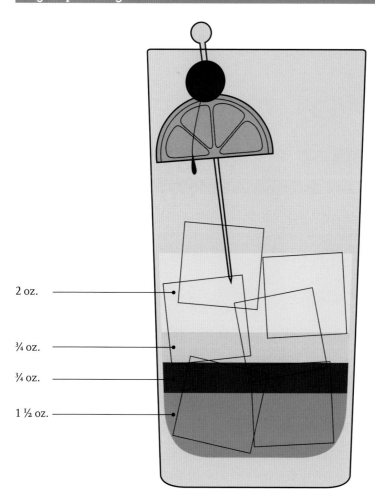

2 oz.

¾ oz.

¾ oz.

1 ½ oz.

INGREDIENTS

KEY

Gin

Cherry Brandy

Lemon Juice

Club Soda

Cherry

Orange

DESCRIPTION

Originally called the "Straits Sling," the Singapore Sling is said to have been developed by Ngiam Tong Boon for the Long Bar in Raffles Hotel in Singapore in the early 1900s. The original recipe created by Boon was lost over time, but was partially recovered by the hotel after gathering recollections from the older bartenders around during that time.

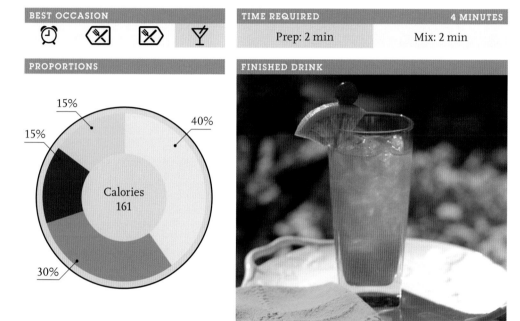

BEST OCCASION

TIME REQUIRED — **4 MINUTES**

Prep: 2 min | Mix: 2 min

PROPORTIONS

15%
15%
40%
Calories 161
30%

FINISHED DRINK

INSTRUCTIONS

1 Combine gin, cherry brandy, and lemon juice in a cocktail shaker. **2** Shake with ice. **3** Strain into a highball glass filled with ice. **4** Pour in the club soda. **5** Garnish with an orange wedge and cherry.

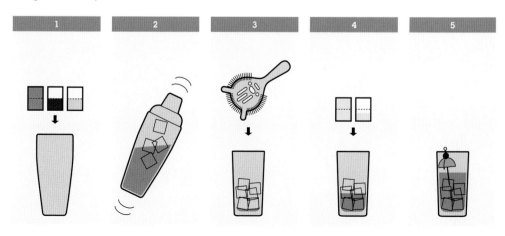

| 1 | 2 | 3 | 4 | 5 |

Tom Collins

tom kol-inz

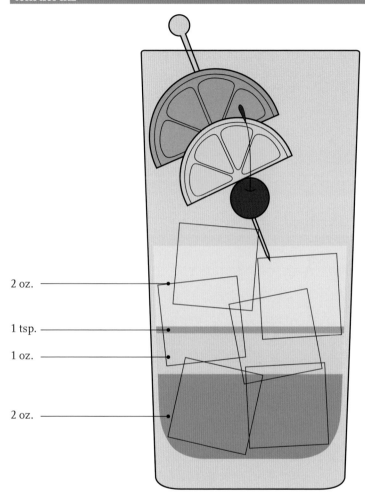

2 oz.

1 tsp.

1 oz.

2 oz.

INGREDIENTS

KEY

- Gin
- Lemon Juice
- Simple Syrup
- Club Soda
- Lemon
- Orange
- Cherry

DESCRIPTION

The Tom Collins came about in 1874 when a rumor spread through New York City that a man by this name had insulted the city and several of its inhabitants and had been seen at various bars in town. When people sought him out, bartenders would serve them "his" drink. A John Collins is made with bourbon, the Juan Collins with tequila, and the Vodka Collins with vodka instead of gin.

BEST OCCASION

TIME REQUIRED — 3 MINUTES

Prep: 2 min | Mix: 1 min

PROPORTIONS

3%
19%
39%
39%

Calories
161

FINISHED DRINK

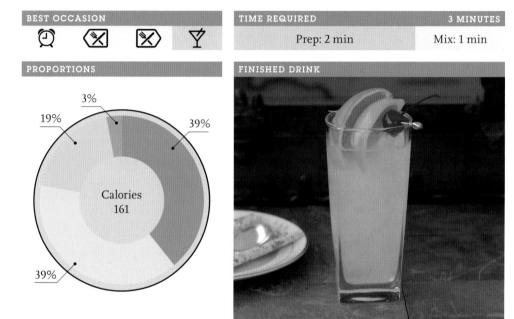

INSTRUCTIONS

1 Combine gin, lemon juice, and simple syrup in a cocktail shaker. 2 Shake with ice. 3 Strain into a highball glass filled with ice. 4 Pour in the club soda. 5 Garnish with a wedge of lemon, a wedge of orange, and a cherry.

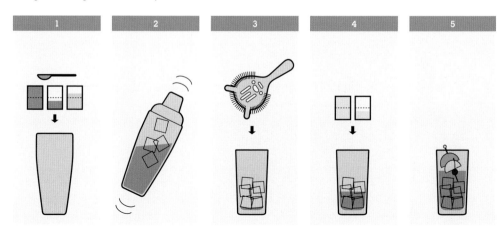

Tuxedo

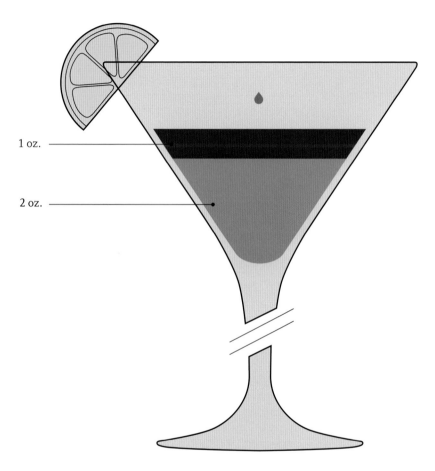

1 oz.

2 oz.

INGREDIENTS

KEY

- Gin
- Dry Sherry
- Orange Bitters
- Lemon

DESCRIPTION

Developed in the late 1800s at the Tuxedo Club in Tuxedo, New York, this drink is a variation of the Martini. The Tuxedo Club was also the birthplace of the tuxedo, when the son of a prominent tobacco tycoon decided to cut off the tails of his dress coat during a ball held at the club.

BEST OCCASION

TIME REQUIRED | 3 MINUTES

Prep: 2 min | Mix: 1 min

PROPORTIONS

1%
33%
66%

Calories
181

FINISHED DRINK

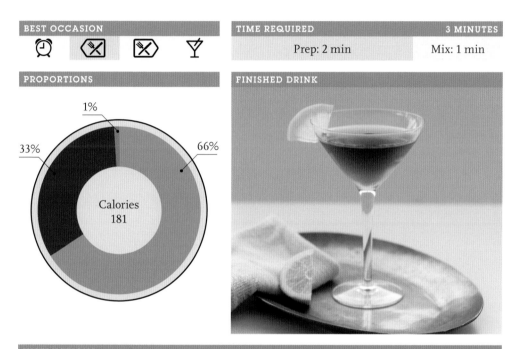

INSTRUCTIONS

1 Combine gin, dry sherry, and orange bitters (1 dash) in a cocktail shaker. **2** Shake with ice. **3** Strain into a chilled cocktail glass. **4** Garnish with a wedge of lemon.

Vesper

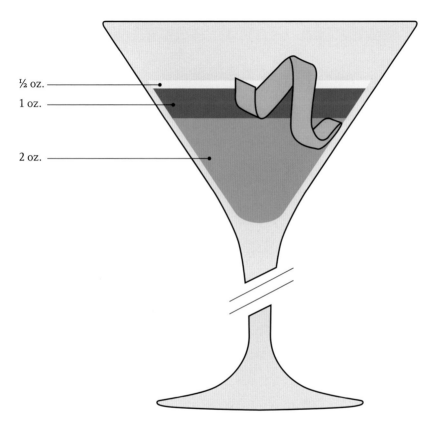

½ oz.

1 oz.

2 oz.

INGREDIENTS

KEY

- Gin
- Vodka
- Lillet Blanc
- Orange

DESCRIPTION

The Vesper is well known as a favorite drink of James Bond in Ian Fleming's 1953 novel, *Casino Royale*. In the novel, James Bond takes credit for creating the drink himself and names it after meeting a beautiful female agent, Vesper Lynd. The drink is said to have been developed by Gilberto Preti at Dukes Hotel in London and first served to Fleming prior to writing *Casino Royale*.

BEST OCCASION

TIME REQUIRED   3 MINUTES

Prep: 2 min   Mix: 1 min

PROPORTIONS

FINISHED DRINK

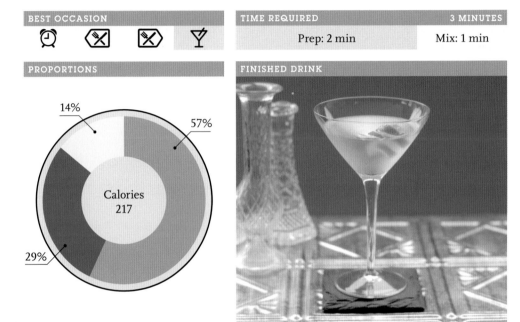

14%

57%

29%

Calories
217

INSTRUCTIONS

1 Combine gin, vodka, and Lillet Blanc in a cocktail shaker. 2 Shake with ice. 3 Strain into a chilled cocktail glass. 4 Garnish with a twist of orange.

Rum

Bahama Mama

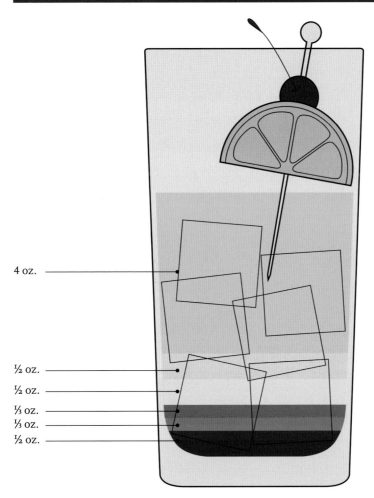

4 oz.

½ oz.
½ oz.
⅓ oz.
⅓ oz.
½ oz.

INGREDIENTS

KEY

■ Dark Rum   ◗ Orange

■ 151-Proof Rum   ● Cherry

■ Coffee Liqueur

□ Coconut Liqueur

□ Lemon Juice

■ Pineapple Juice

DESCRIPTION

The Bahama Mama is a fruity tropical drink that is perfect for vacations and hot summer afternoons. Fresh ingredients, particularly fruit juices, make this cocktail extra special.

BEST OCCASION

TIME REQUIRED   3 MINUTES

Prep: 2 min   Mix: 1 min

PROPORTIONS

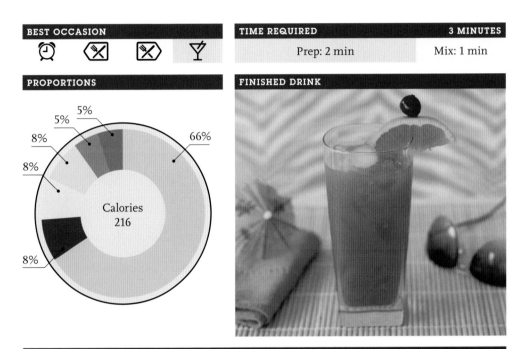

5%
5%
8%
8%
66%
Calories
216
8%

FINISHED DRINK

INSTRUCTIONS

1 Combine dark rum, 151-proof rum, coffee liqueur, coconut liqueur, lemon juice, and pineapple juice in a cocktail shaker. **2** Shake with ice. **3** Strain into a highball glass filled with ice. **4** Garnish with an orange wedge and cherry.

1   2   3   4

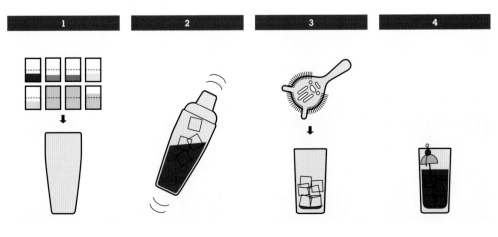

Blue Hawaiian

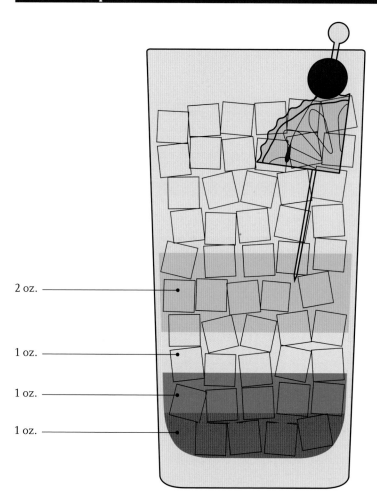

2 oz.

1 oz.

1 oz.

1 oz.

INGREDIENTS

KEY

- Light Rum
- Blue Curaçao
- Coconut Cream
- Pineapple Juice
- Pineapple
- Cherry

DESCRIPTION

Essentially a blue Piña Colada, the Blue Hawaiian is enjoyed both blended and over ice. Many believe the drink was first created by Ernest Gantt, famously known as "Don the Beachcomber," an entrepreneur of Tiki-inspired restaurants and bars. Gantt and Victor Bergeron, known as "Trader Vic" (also a Tiki-themed restaurant entrepreneur), were amicable rivals for a number of years.

BEST OCCASION

TIME REQUIRED   5 MINUTES

Prep: 2 min	Mix: 3 min

PROPORTIONS

FINISHED DRINK

20%
40%
Calories
274
20%
20%
20%

INSTRUCTIONS

1 Combine light rum, blue curaçao, coconut cream, and pineapple juice in a blender with ice.
2 Blend. **3** Pour into a highball glass. **4** Garnish with a pineapple wedge and cherry (optional).

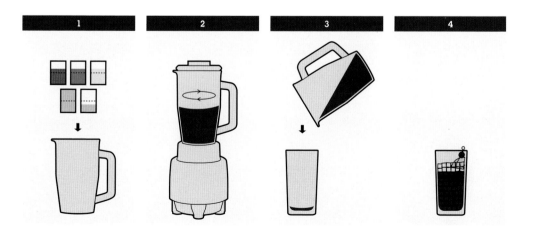

Caipirinha

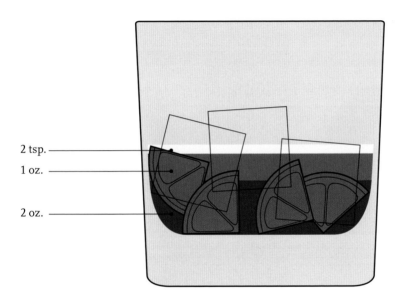

2 tsp.
1 oz.
2 oz.

INGREDIENTS

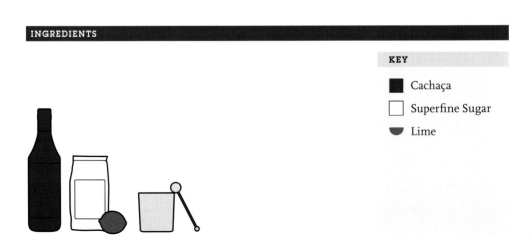

KEY

■ Cachaça
□ Superfine Sugar
◗ Lime

DESCRIPTION

The Caipirinha is a traditional Brazilian cocktail whose literal translation is "little country bumpkin." The key ingredient in this cocktail is the cachaça, a Brazilian spirit made from sugarcane juice. The Caipirinha is the national drink of Brazil and is a favorite during Carnaval. Try substituting cachaça with light rum.

BEST OCCASION

TIME REQUIRED   4 MINUTES

Prep: 2 min	Mix: 2 min

PROPORTIONS

FINISHED DRINK

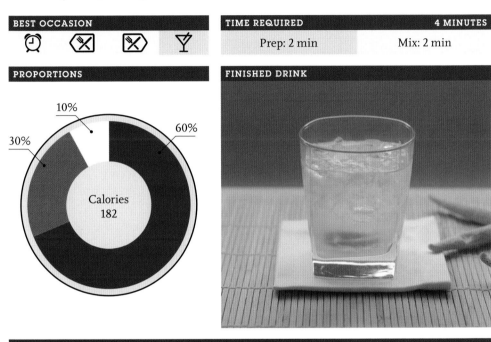

10%
30%
60%
Calories
182

INSTRUCTIONS

1 Add lime wedges (1 lime, quartered) and superfine sugar to a rocks glass. **2** Muddle until sugar dissolves. **3** Add ice and cachaça. **4** Stir well.

1	2	3	4

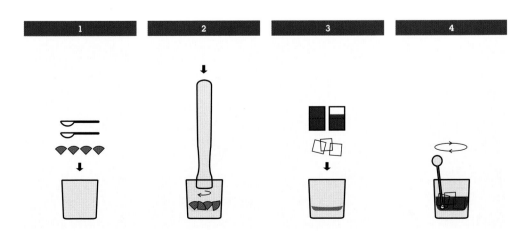

Cuba Libre

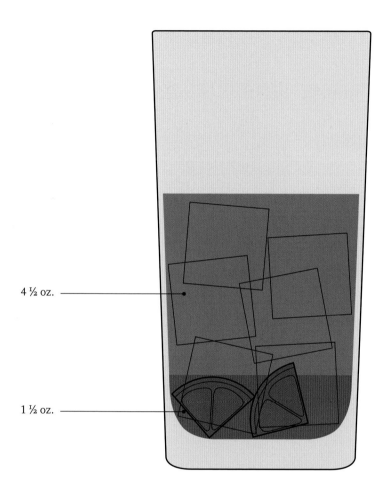

4 ½ oz.

1 ½ oz.

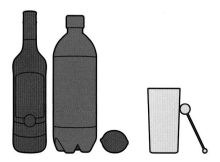

KEY

- Light Rum
- Cola
- Lime

DESCRIPTION

As the story goes, during Cuba's War of Independence with Spain in the late 1800s, an American was spotted drinking Bacardi Rum and Coca-Cola by a group of American soldiers at a bar in Havana. The soldiers tried the drink and asked what it was called. It had no name, so the soldiers decided to call it a "Cuba Libre," or translated, "free Cuba."

BEST OCCASION

TIME REQUIRED   2½ MINUTES

Prep: 2 min   Mix: 30 sec

PROPORTIONS

FINISHED DRINK

8%
69%
Calories
166
23%

INSTRUCTIONS

1 Pour light rum and cola into a highball glass filled with ice. **2** Squeeze the juice from two lime wedges into the drink. **3** Stir well.

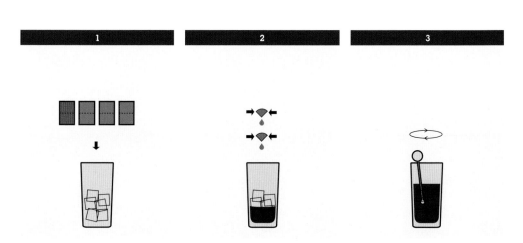

1   2   3

Daiquiri

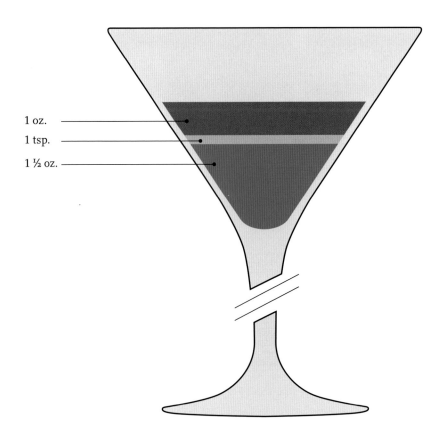

1 oz.

1 tsp.

1 ½ oz.

INGREDIENTS

KEY

- Light Rum
- Simple Syrup
- Lime Juice

DESCRIPTION

The Daiquiri is often credited to American Jennings Cox, who is said to have invented it with fellow iron-ore miners while working near the town of Daiquiri, Cuba, in 1905. The recipe eventually made it back to the U.S., carried by a U.S. admiral, who introduced the cocktail to the U.S. in Washington, D.C. For a Frozen Daiquiri, combine ingredients in a blender with ice along with desired fruit.

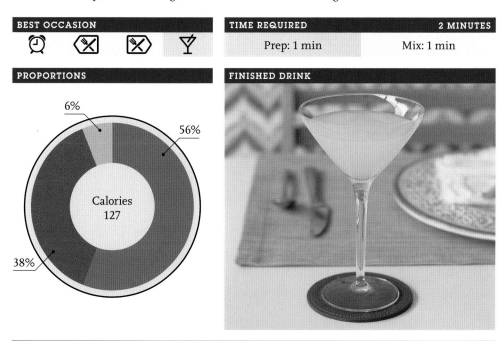

BEST OCCASION

TIME REQUIRED — **2 MINUTES**
Prep: 1 min   Mix: 1 min

PROPORTIONS

6%
56%
38%
Calories 127

FINISHED DRINK

INSTRUCTIONS

1 Combine light rum, simple syrup, and lime juice in a shaker. **2** Shake with ice. **3** Strain into a chilled cocktail glass.

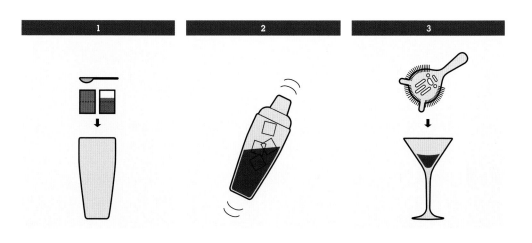

1   2   3

Dark & Stormy

dahrk aynd stawr-mee

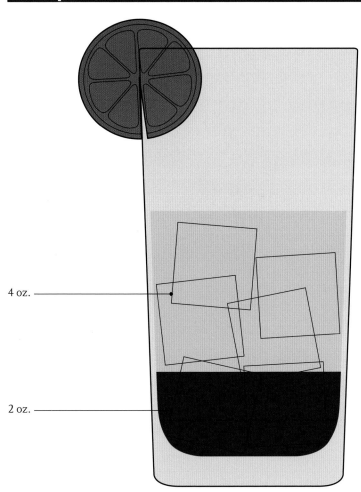

4 oz.

2 oz.

INGREDIENTS

Dark Rum

Ginger Beer

Lime

DESCRIPTION

The Dark & Stormy is the national drink of Bermuda, where Gosling's rum and ginger beer are made. According to Gosling's, there was an old ginger-beer factory that was run by the British Naval Officers' Club. The sailors soon began adding Gosling's Black Seal Rum to their ginger beer. The drink was named after a sailor remarked it was "the color of a cloud only a fool or dead man would sail under."

BEST OCCASION

TIME REQUIRED — 2½ MINUTES

Prep: 2 min   Mix: 30 sec

PROPORTIONS

33%   66%

Calories
202

FINISHED DRINK

INSTRUCTIONS

1 Pour dark rum and ginger beer into a highball glass filled with ice. **2** Garnish with a lime wheel.

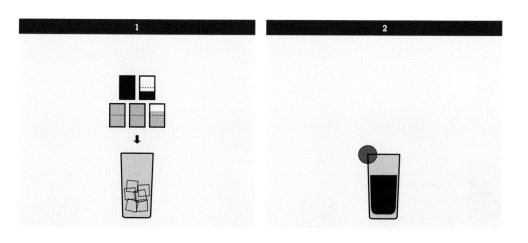

Fog Cutter

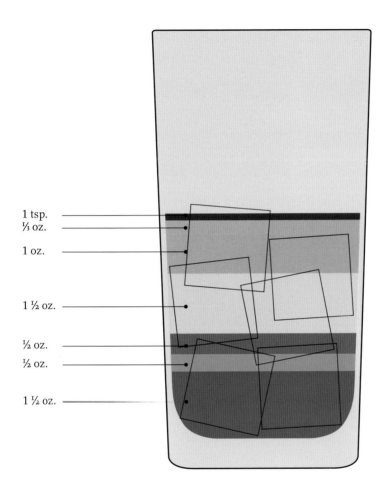

1 tsp.
⅓ oz.
1 oz.

1 ½ oz.

½ oz.
½ oz.

1 ½ oz.

INGREDIENTS

KEY

- Light Rum
- Gin
- Brandy
- Lemon Juice
- Orange Juice
- Orgeat Syrup
- Sweet Sherry

DESCRIPTION

Victor Bergeron, or "Trader Vic" as he became known, a Tiki-inspired restaurant entrepreneur, claimed to have invented the Fog Cutter. Vic is famously quoted as saying, "Fog Cutter, hell. After two of these, you won't even see the stuff."

BEST OCCASION

TIME REQUIRED   3 MINUTES

Prep: 1 min   Mix: 2 min

PROPORTIONS

FINISHED DRINK

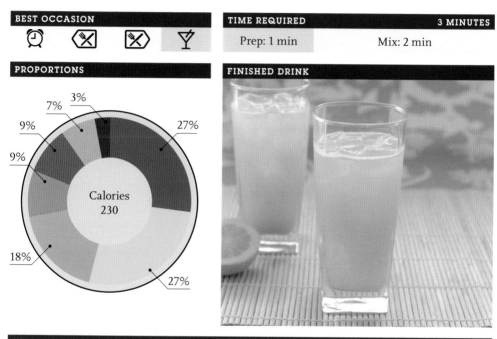

Calories 230

3% · 7% · 9% · 9% · 27% · 27% · 18%

INSTRUCTIONS

1 Combine light rum, gin, brandy, lemon juice, orange juice, and orgeat syrup in a cocktail shaker. **2** Shake with ice. **3** Strain into a highball glass filled with ice. **4** Top with sweet sherry.

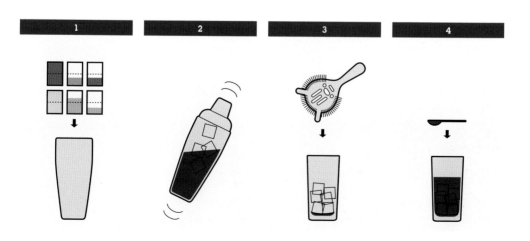

Hurricane

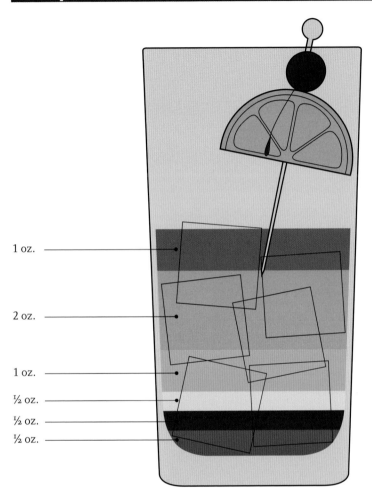

1 oz.

2 oz.

1 oz.

½ oz.

½ oz.

½ oz.

INGREDIENTS

KEY

Light Rum	Orange
Dark Rum	Cherry
Galliano	
Pineapple Juice	
Orange Juice	
Lime Juice	

DESCRIPTION

Named after the hurricane-lamp-shaped glasses the drinks were first served in, the Hurricane was purportedly created at Pat O'Brien's bar in the 1940s in New Orleans. The story goes that O'Brien created the drink as a means of liquidating excessive stock of rum his distributors forced him to purchase. Try adding a splash of grenadine to deepen the drink's color.

BEST OCCASION

TIME REQUIRED   3 ½ MINUTES

Prep: 2 min	Mix: 1 ½ min

PROPORTIONS

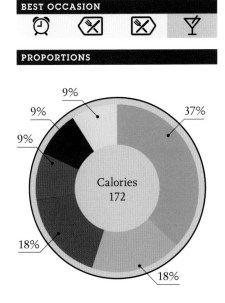

9%
9%
9%
9%
37%
Calories
172
18%
18%

FINISHED DRINK

INSTRUCTIONS

1 Combine light rum, dark rum, Galliano, pineapple juice, orange juice, and lime juice in a cocktail shaker. **2** Shake with ice. **3** Strain into a highball glass filled with ice. **4** Garnish with an orange slice and cherry.

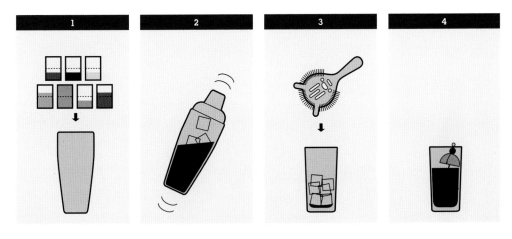

| 1 | 2 | 3 | 4 |

Mai Tai

mahy tahy

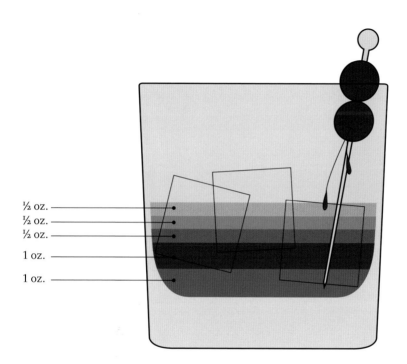

½ oz. —————
½ oz. —————
½ oz. —————
1 oz. —————
1 oz. —————

INGREDIENTS

KEY

- Light Rum
- Dark Rum
- Lime Juice
- Orange Curaçao
- Orgeat Syrup
- Cherry

DESCRIPTION

Trader Vic, the father of the Fog Cutter, created the Mai Tai in 1944 for his Tiki restaurants. According to Vic, he concocted the drink one afternoon for friends visiting from Tahiti. After tasting it, one of those friends exclaimed, "Maita'i roa ae!"—meaning "Out of this world!" Vic, liking the sound of it, decided to name the drink the Mai Tai.

BEST OCCASION

TIME REQUIRED   3 MINUTES

Prep: 1 min   Mix: 2 min

PROPORTIONS

FINISHED DRINK

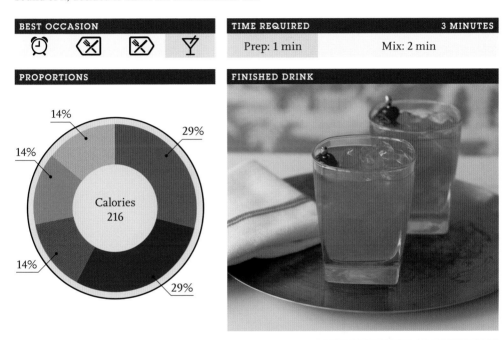

14%
29%
14%
14%

Calories
216

14%
29%

INSTRUCTIONS

1 Combine light rum, dark rum, lime juice, orange curaçao, and orgeat syrup in a cocktail shaker. **2** Shake with ice. **3** Strain into a rocks glass filled with ice. **4** Garnish with cherries.

| 1 | 2 | 3 | 4 |

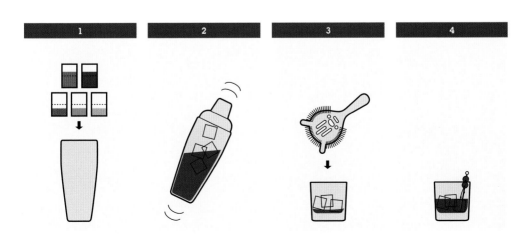

Mojito

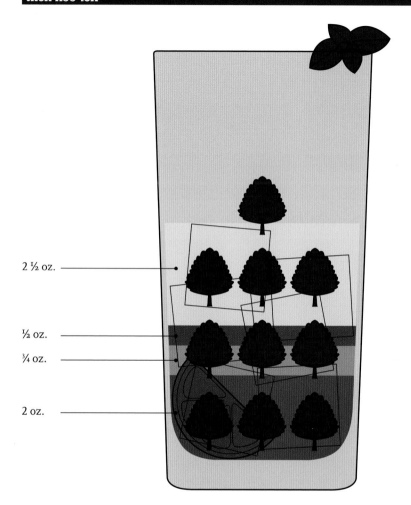

2 ½ oz.

½ oz.

¾ oz.

2 oz.

KEY

- Light Rum
- Simple Syrup
- Club Soda
- Lime
- Mint Sprigs

DESCRIPTION

Considered to be the Mint Julep's Cuban cousin, the Mojito originated in Havana and was one of Ernest Hemingway's favorite cocktails. While the origins of the drink are subject to debate, Sir Francis Drake is often credited with creating a similar cocktail using aguardiente, a primitive predecessor to rum, in the sixteenth century.

BEST OCCASION

TIME REQUIRED · 4 MINUTES

Prep: 2 min | Mix: 2 min

PROPORTIONS

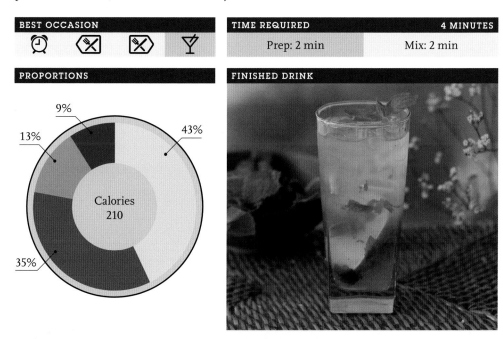

9%
13%
43%
35%
Calories 210

FINISHED DRINK

INSTRUCTIONS

1 Place mint leaves and simple syrup into a highball glass with juice of half a lime. **2** Muddle the ingredients. **3** Add ice and light rum. **4** Stir well. **5** Top with club soda.

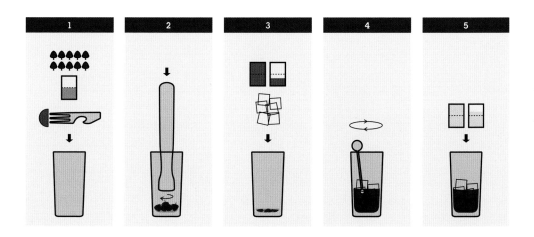

Painkiller

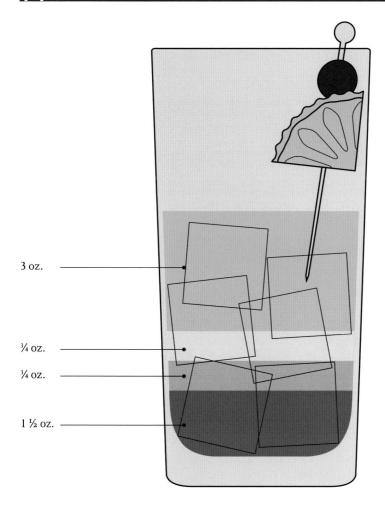

3 oz.

¾ oz.

¾ oz.

1 ½ oz.

INGREDIENTS

KEY

- Light Rum
- Orange Juice
- Coconut Cream
- Pineapple Juice
- Pineapple
- Cherry

DESCRIPTION

Cocktail lore has it that the Painkiller was invented at the Soggy Dollar Bar in the British Virgin Islands. Because the island had no dock and most customers were sailors, they would swim to shore and pay with wet dollars, giving the bar its distinctive name.

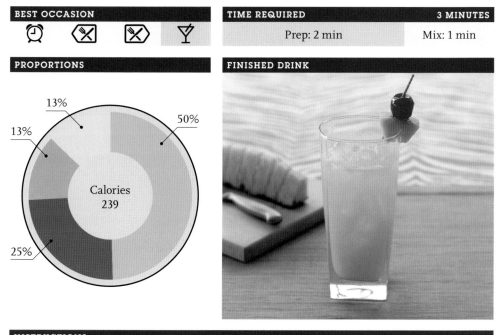

BEST OCCASION

TIME REQUIRED — **3 MINUTES**

Prep: 2 min | Mix: 1 min

PROPORTIONS

13% · 13% · 50% · 25% · Calories 239

FINISHED DRINK

INSTRUCTIONS

1 Combine light rum, orange juice, coconut cream, and pineapple juice in a cocktail shaker. **2** Shake with ice. **3** Strain into a highball glass filled with ice. **4** Garnish with a pineapple wedge and cherry.

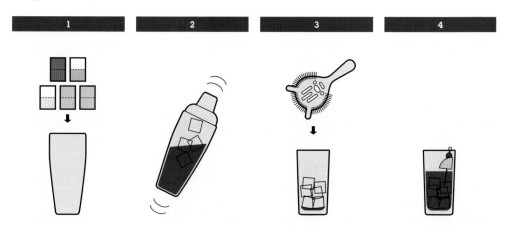

Piña Colada

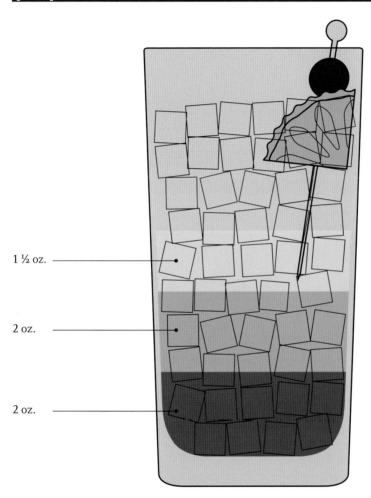

1 ½ oz.

2 oz.

2 oz.

INGREDIENTS

KEY

- Light Rum
- Pineapple Juice
- Coconut Cream
- Pineapple
- Cherry

DESCRIPTION

The Piña Colada (translated "strained pineapple") has been the national drink of Puerto Rico since 1978. The cocktail was likely created at the Caribe Hilton's Beachcomber Bar by bartender Ramon Marrero Perez in 1954. The hotel asked Perez to create a new signature drink for their patrons. This story is confirmed in the book *Puerto Rico: La Gran Cocina del Caribe* by Jose Luiz Dias de Villegas.

BEST OCCASION

TIME REQUIRED   5 MINUTES

Prep: 2 min   Mix: 3 min

PROPORTIONS

FINISHED DRINK

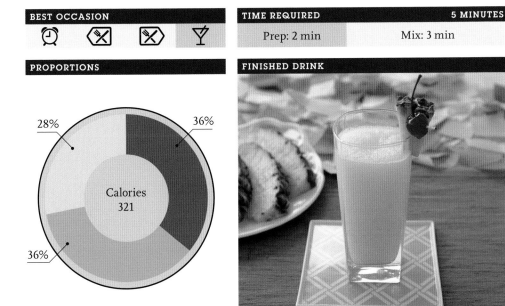

28%   36%
36%

Calories
321

INSTRUCTIONS

1 Combine ice, light rum, pineapple juice, and coconut cream in a blender with ice. **2** Blend.
3 Pour into a highball glass. **4** Garnish with a pineapple wedge and cherry.

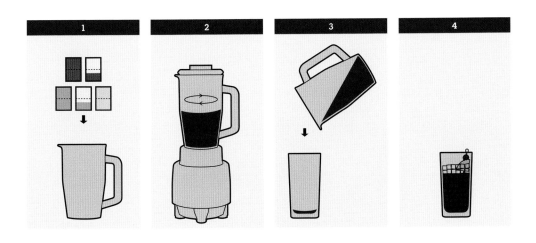

Planter's Punch

plan-ters puhnch

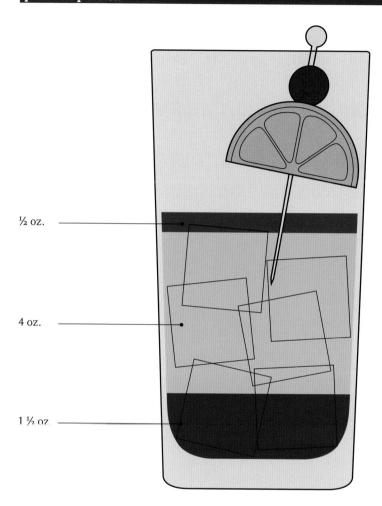

½ oz.

4 oz.

1 ½ oz.

INGREDIENTS

KEY

■ Dark Jamaican Rum

▨ Pineapple Juice

■ Grenadine

● Cherry

◡ Orange

DESCRIPTION

A classic rum drink, the Planter's Punch was created in the late nineteenth century, perhaps by Fred L. Myers, the founder of Myers's Jamaican rum. A recipe for the drink appears in an 1878 issue of the weekly London magazine *Fun*.

BEST OCCASION

TIME REQUIRED   3 MINUTES

Prep: 2 min	Mix: 1 min

PROPORTIONS

FINISHED DRINK

8%
25%
67%

Calories
209

INSTRUCTIONS

1 Combine dark Jamaican rum, pineapple juice, and grenadine in a cocktail shaker.
2 Shake with ice. **3** Strain into a highball glass filled with ice. **4** Garnish with an orange wedge and cherry.

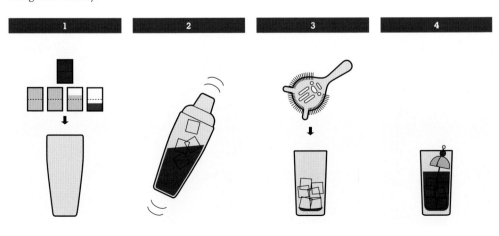

Rum Runner

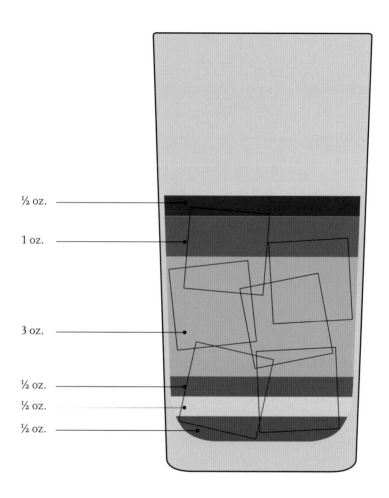

½ oz.

1 oz.

3 oz.

½ oz.

½ oz.

½ oz.

INGREDIENTS

KEY

- Light Rum
- Banana Liqueur
- Chambord
- Pineapple Juice
- Lime Juice
- Grenadine

DESCRIPTION

Bursting with fruit flavor, the Rum Runner is a very popular rum drink. As the story goes, the cocktail was invented in the 1950s at the Holiday Isle Tiki Bar in Islamorada, Florida, when the bar had excessive inventory of rum and liqueurs. The drink is named after "rum-runners"—smugglers of alcohol over the water (particularly popular during Prohibition)—who once inhabited the Florida Keys.

BEST OCCASION

TIME REQUIRED — 2 MINUTES

Prep: 1 min   Mix: 1 min

PROPORTIONS

FINISHED DRINK

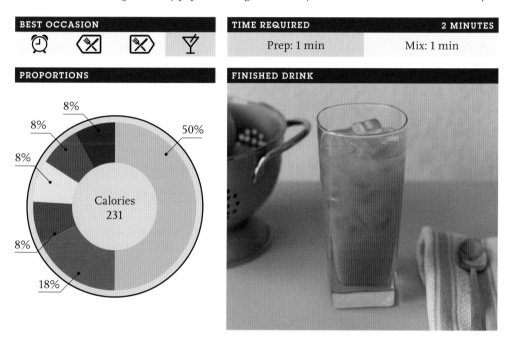

8%
8%
8%
50%
Calories
231
8%
18%

INSTRUCTIONS

1 Combine light rum, banana liqueur, Chambord, pineapple juice, lime juice, and grenadine in a cocktail shaker. **2** Shake with ice. **3** Strain into a highball glass filled with ice.

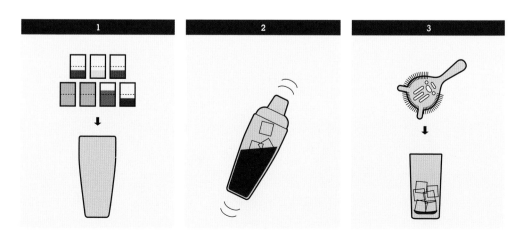

Zombie

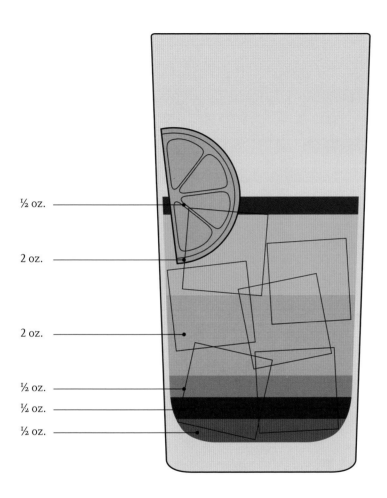

½ oz.

2 oz.

2 oz.

½ oz.

½ oz.

½ oz.

INGREDIENTS

KEY

- Light Rum
- Dark Rum
- Triple Sec
- Orange Juice
- Pineapple Juice
- Grenadine
- Orange

DESCRIPTION

The Zombie's creation is credited to Ernest Gantt, otherwise known as "Don the Beachcomber," who created the cocktail in the late 1930s. The Zombie later made its international debut after being introduced in 1939 at the World's Fair. The drink's name comes from the cocktail's effect on its drinkers—making them feel like zombies after consumption.

BEST OCCASION

TIME REQUIRED | **3 MINUTES**

Prep: 2 min | Mix: 1 min

PROPORTIONS

FINISHED DRINK

8%
8%
8%
34%
Calories
220
8%
34%

INSTRUCTIONS

1 Combine light rum, dark rum, triple sec, orange juice, pineapple juice, and grenadine in a cocktail shaker. **2** Shake with ice. **3** Strain into a highball glass filled with ice. **4** Garnish with an orange wedge.

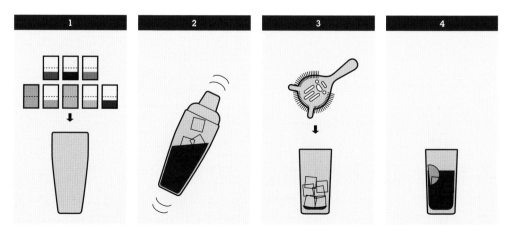

Tequila

Acapulco

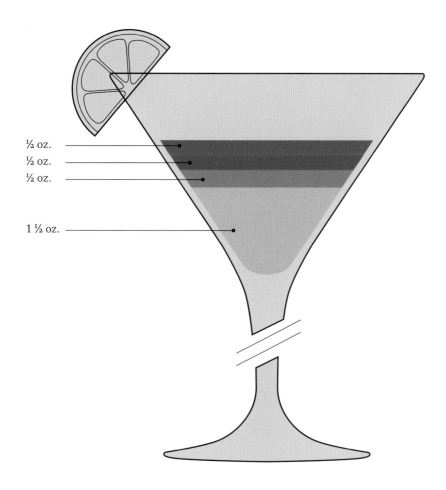

½ oz.
½ oz.
½ oz.

1 ½ oz.

INGREDIENTS

KEY

Gold Tequila

Triple Sec

Light Rum

Lime Juice

Lemon

DESCRIPTION

The Acapulco is a fruity drink with a nice balance between tequila and rum. The cocktail is named after the beach-lined city on the west coast of Mexico.

BEST OCCASION

TIME REQUIRED — 3 MINUTES

Prep: 2 min | Mix: 1 min

PROPORTIONS

17%
50%
17%
Calories
194
17%

FINISHED DRINK

INSTRUCTIONS

1 Combine gold tequila, triple sec, light rum, and lime juice in a cocktail shaker. 2 Shake with ice. 3 Strain into a chilled cocktail glass. 4 Garnish with a lemon wedge.

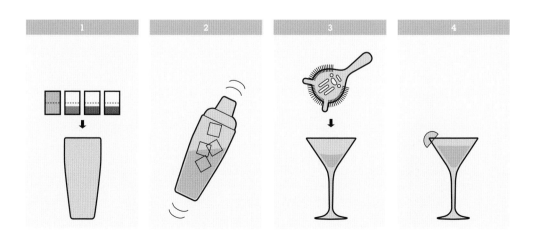

Brave Bull

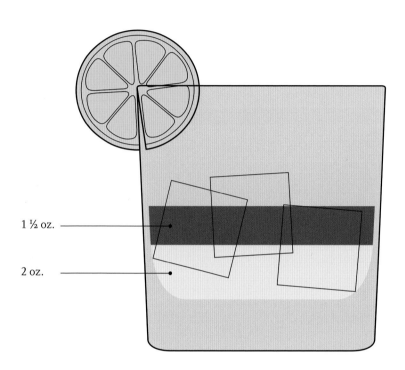

1 ½ oz.

2 oz.

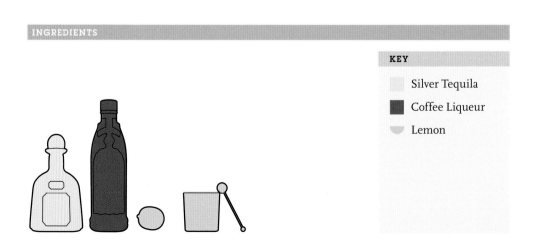

KEY

Silver Tequila

Coffee Liqueur

Lemon

The tequila cousin of the vodka-based Black Russian, the Brave Bull is a classic tequila cocktail that is surprisingly smooth and tastes like chocolate cake.

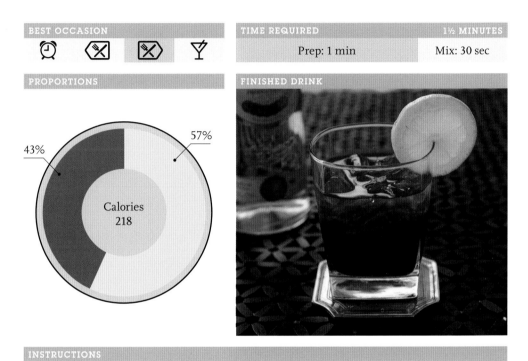

BEST OCCASION

TIME REQUIRED — 1½ MINUTES

Prep: 1 min | Mix: 30 sec

PROPORTIONS

FINISHED DRINK

57%

43%

Calories
218

INSTRUCTIONS

1 Pour silver tequila and coffee liqueur into a rocks glass with ice. 2 Stir well. 3 Garnish with a lemon wheel.

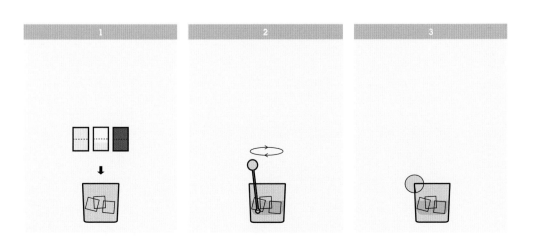

Freddie Fudpucker

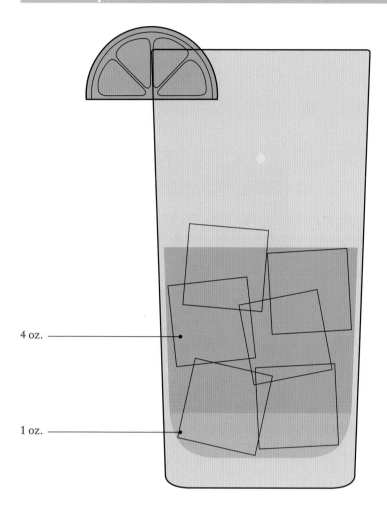

4 oz.

1 oz.

INGREDIENTS

KEY

Tequila

Orange Juice

Galliano

Orange

DESCRIPTION

The Freddie Fudpucker, also called a Cactus Banger, is essentially a Harvey Wallbanger made with tequila instead of vodka. This drink will send you back to bed in the morning.

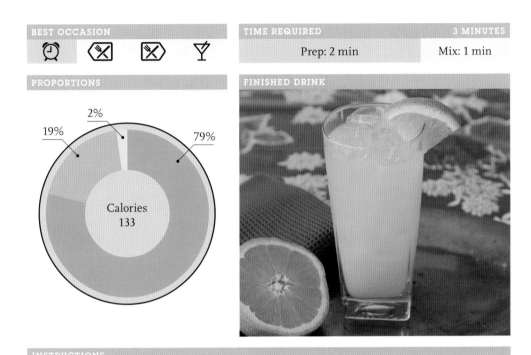

BEST OCCASION

TIME REQUIRED   3 MINUTES

Prep: 2 min   Mix: 1 min

PROPORTIONS

2%
19%
79%
Calories
133

FINISHED DRINK

INSTRUCTIONS

1 Pour tequila and orange juice into a highball glass with ice cubes. 2 Stir well. 3 Float Galliano on top. 4 Garnish with an orange wedge.

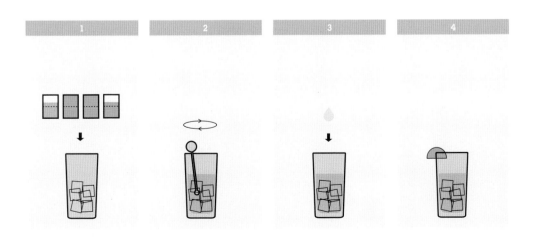

Margarita

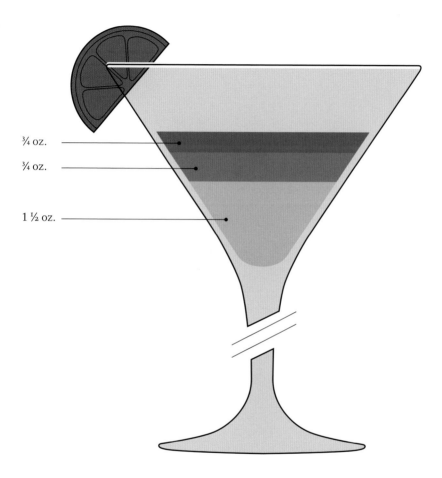

¾ oz.

¾ oz.

1 ½ oz.

INGREDIENTS

KEY

- Tequila
- Triple Sec
- Lime Juice
- Lime
- Salt

DESCRIPTION

The Margarita, which is Spanish for "daisy," is one of the most popular cocktails in the U.S. and easily the most common tequila-based drink. While there are many stories surrounding its origin, the Margarita was, by all accounts, created in the 1930s in Mexico. Try blending the Margarita with ice for a Frozen Margarita.

BEST OCCASION

TIME REQUIRED   3½ MINUTES

Prep: 2 ½ min   Mix: 1 min

PROPORTIONS

FINISHED DRINK

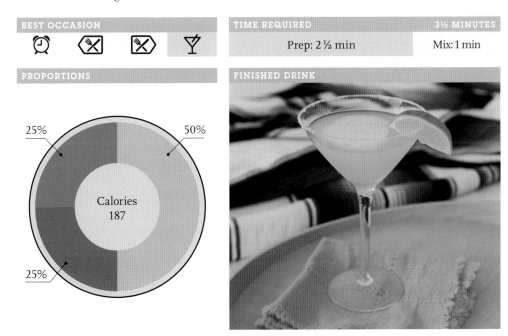

25%   50%

Calories
187

25%

INSTRUCTIONS

1 Apply salt to a wet cocktail-glass rim. 2 Combine tequila, triple sec, and lime juice in a shaker. 3 Shake with ice. 4 Strain into a chilled cocktail glass. 5 Garnish with a wedge of lime.

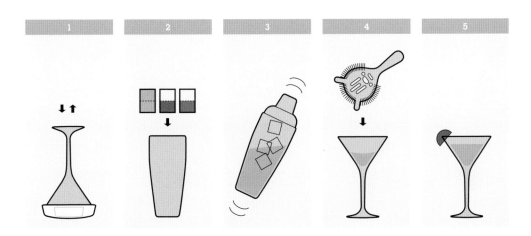

Matador

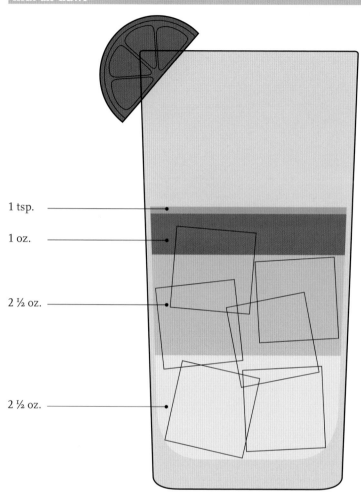

1 tsp.

1 oz.

2 ½ oz.

2 ½ oz.

INGREDIENTS

KEY

- Silver Tequila
- Pineapple Juice
- Lime Juice
- Simple Syrup
- Lime

DESCRIPTION

The Matador is similar in structure to the Margarita, with the exception of the added pineapple juice, which helps to give the Mexican drink a pleasant tropical infusion.

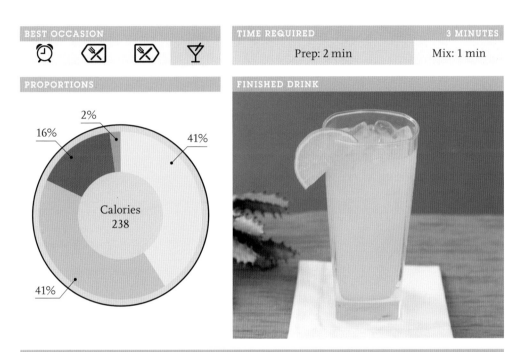

BEST OCCASION

TIME REQUIRED — 3 MINUTES

Prep: 2 min | Mix: 1 min

PROPORTIONS

2%
16%
41%
41%

Calories
238

FINISHED DRINK

INSTRUCTIONS

1 Combine silver tequila, pineapple juice, lime juice, and simple syrup in a cocktail shaker.

2 Shake with ice. 3 Strain into a highball glass filled with ice. 4 Garnish with a lime wedge.

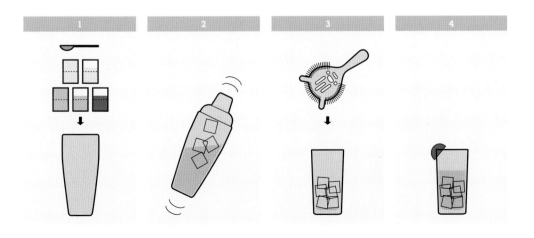

1 | 2 | 3 | 4

Paloma

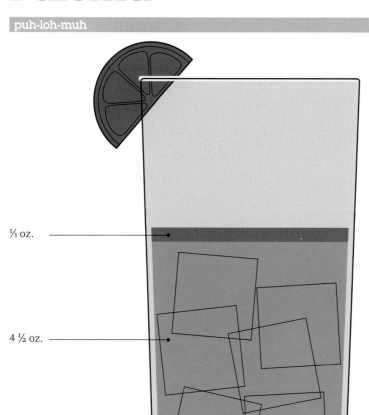

⅓ oz.

4 ½ oz.

1 ½ oz.

INGREDIENTS

KEY

- Silver Tequila
- Grapefruit Soda
- Lime Juice
- Lime
- Salt

The Paloma, meaning "dove" in Spanish, is a very popular drink in Mexico. The cocktail is considered to be one of the smoothest tequila drinks.

Prep: 2 min   Mix: 1 min

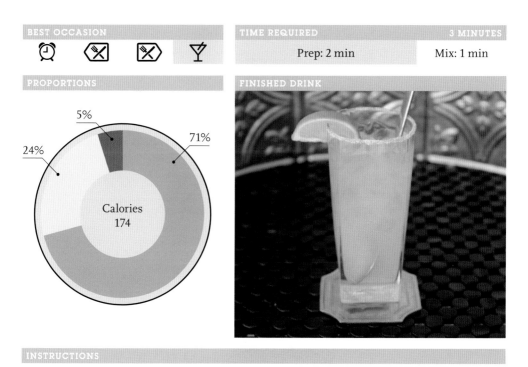

5%

71%

24%

Calories
174

1 Apply salt to a wet highball glass rim. 2 Pour silver tequila, grapefruit soda, and lime juice into a highball glass with ice cubes. 3 Garnish with a lime wedge.

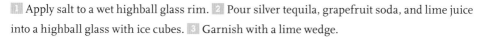

1   2   3

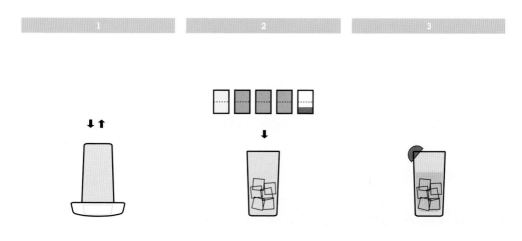

Tequila Sunrise

tuh-kee-luh suhn-rahyz

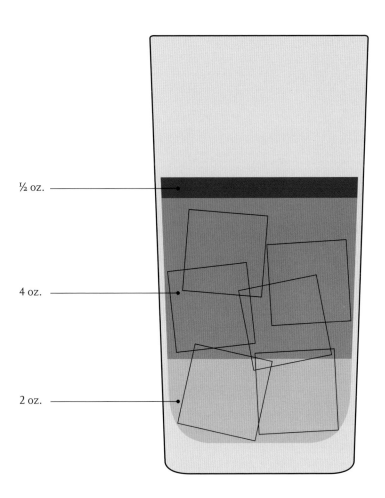

½ oz.

4 oz.

2 oz.

INGREDIENTS

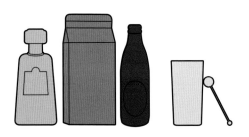

KEY

- Tequila
- Orange Juice
- Grenadine

DESCRIPTION

The Tequila Sunrise was first served in Acapulco and Cancun in the 1950s and gained mainstream popularity in the 1970s. The drink is named after the sunrise effect created by allowing the grenadine to slowly settle at the bottom of the glass.

BEST OCCASION

TIME REQUIRED   **2 MINUTES**

Prep: 1 min   Mix: 1 min

PROPORTIONS

FINISHED DRINK

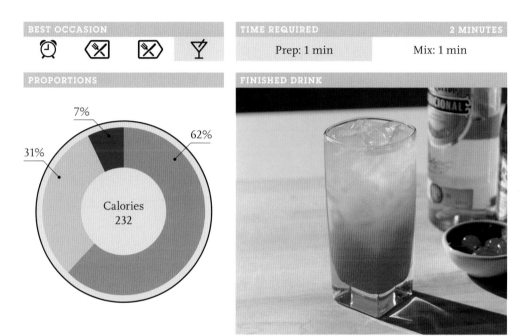

7%

62%

31%

Calories
232

INSTRUCTIONS

1 Pour tequila and orange juice into a highball glass with ice. 2 Stir well. 3 Drip the grenadine into the glass slowly.

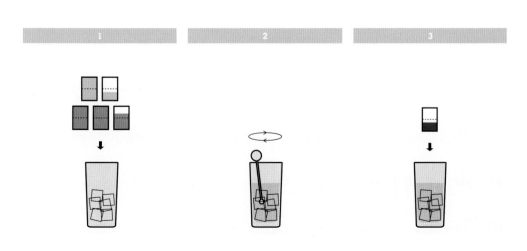

Tequila Sunset

tuh-kee-luh suhn-set

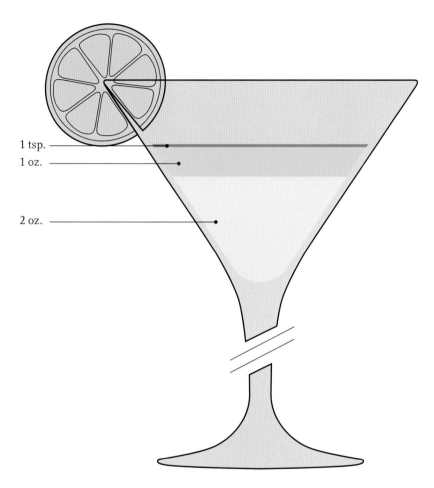

1 tsp. ————

1 oz. ————

2 oz. ————

KEY

Silver Tequila

Lemon Juice

Clear Honey

Lemon

DESCRIPTION

While not as visually striking as the Tequila Sunrise, the Tequila Sunset is an interesting drink that combines sweet and sour with the smoothness of honey.

BEST OCCASION

TIME REQUIRED · 3 MINUTES

| Prep: 2 min | Mix: 1 min |

PROPORTIONS

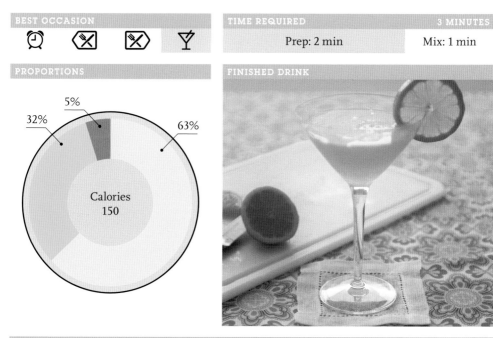

5%
32%
63%
Calories
150

FINISHED DRINK

INSTRUCTIONS

1 Combine silver tequila, lemon juice, and clear honey in a cocktail shaker. **2** Shake with ice. **3** Strain into a chilled cocktail glass. **4** Garnish with a lemon wheel.

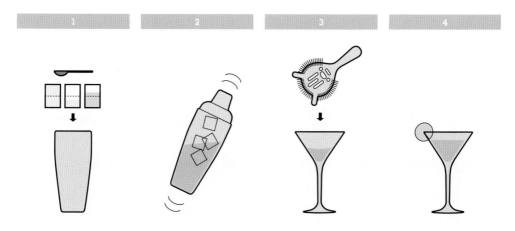

1 2 3 4

Tequini

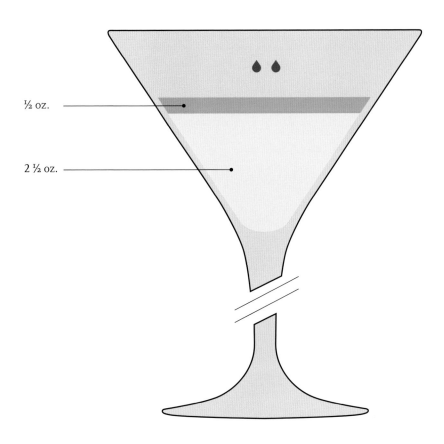

½ oz.

2 ½ oz.

INGREDIENTS

KEY

- Silver Tequila
- Dry Vermouth
- Angostura Bitters

DESCRIPTION

The Mexican equivalent of a Martini, the Tequini is a unique dry tequila drink. Try substituting silver tequila and dry vermouth with gold tequila and sweet vermouth to sweeten the cocktail.

BEST OCCASION

TIME REQUIRED — 2 MINUTES

Prep: 1 min   Mix: 1 min

PROPORTIONS

3%
16%
81%

Calories
200

FINISHED DRINK

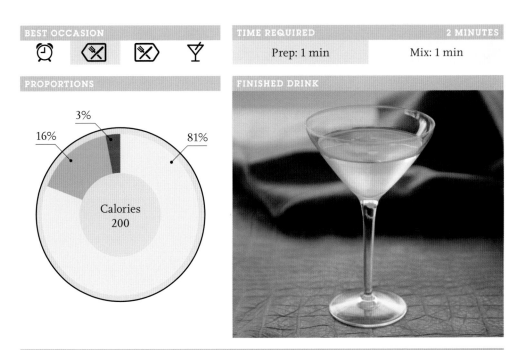

INSTRUCTIONS

1 Combine silver tequila, dry vermouth, and Angostura bitters (2 dashes) in a shaker. 2 Shake with ice. 3 Strain into a chilled cocktail glass.

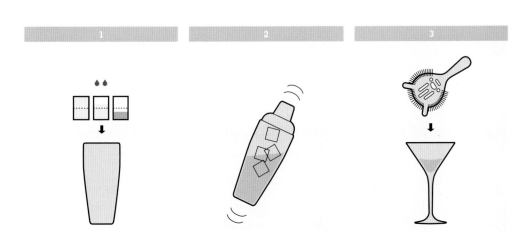

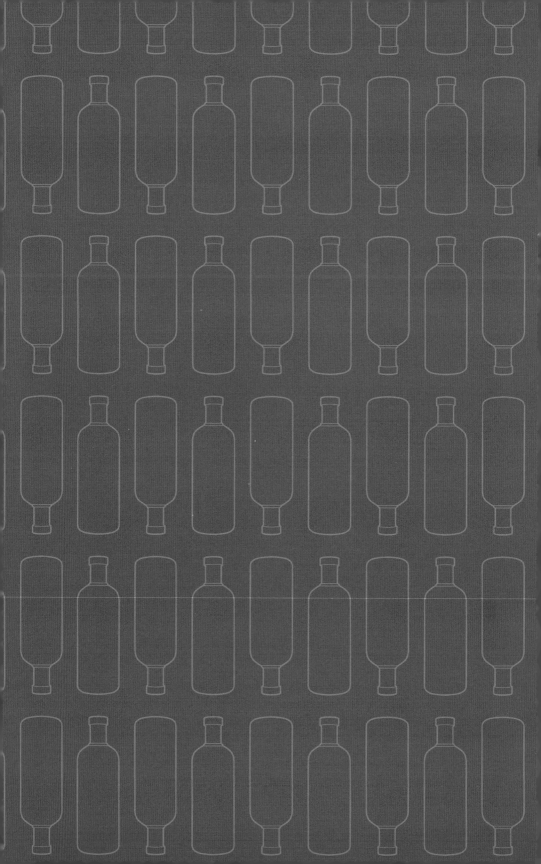

Vodka

Alabama Slammer

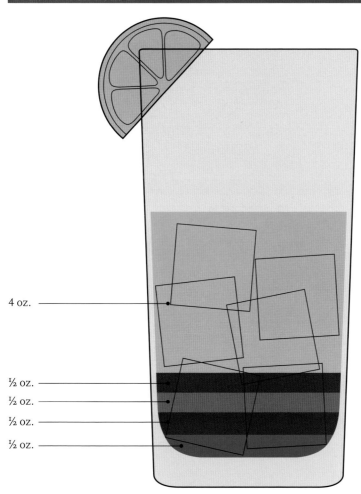

4 oz.

½ oz.
½ oz.
½ oz.
½ oz.

INGREDIENTS

KEY

- Vodka
- Southern Comfort
- Amaretto
- Sloe Gin
- Orange Juice
- Orange

DESCRIPTION

The Alabama Slammer is a refreshing cocktail that goes down easy. Along with the rest of the ingredients, the combination of orange juice, Southern Comfort, and amaretto is magical. Sloe gin is a liqueur flavored with sloe berries, a small fruit that is closely related to the plum.

BEST OCCASION

TIME REQUIRED   2½ MINUTES

Prep: 2 min   Mix: 30 sec

PROPORTIONS

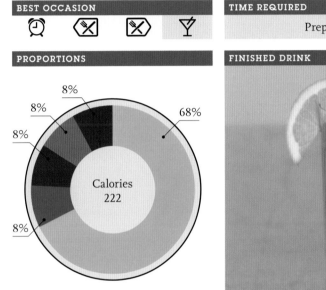

8%
8%
8%
68%
Calories
222
8%

FINISHED DRINK

INSTRUCTIONS

1 Pour vodka, Southern Comfort, amaretto, sloe gin, and orange juice into a highball glass with ice cubes. **2** Stir well. **3** Garnish with an orange wedge.

1	2	3

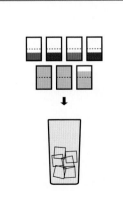

Appletini

ap-uhl-tee-nee

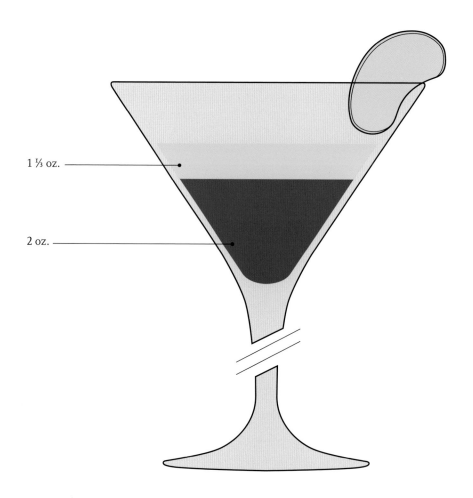

1 ⅓ oz.

2 oz.

INGREDIENTS

KEY

■ Vodka

■ Apple Schnapps

■ Green Apple

DESCRIPTION

The Appletini, also known as an Apple Martini, is becoming increasingly popular in metropolitan areas across the U.S. and is a nice alternative for Cosmopolitan drinkers. Try adding a touch of triple sec for increased depth of flavor.

BEST OCCASION

TIME REQUIRED   3 MINUTES

Prep: 2 min   Mix: 1 min

PROPORTIONS

40%   60%

Calories
234

FINISHED DRINK

INSTRUCTIONS

1 Combine vodka and apple schnapps in a cocktail shaker. **2** Shake with ice. **3** Strain into a chilled cocktail glass. **4** Garnish with an apple slice.

| 1 | 2 | 3 | 4 |

Black Magic

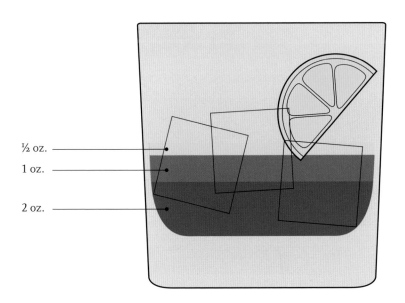

½ oz.
1 oz.
2 oz.

INGREDIENTS

- Vodka
- Coffee Liqueur
- Lemon Juice
- Lemon

DESCRIPTION

With a name fit for Halloween parties, the Black Magic is essentially a Black Russian with lemon juice added. The lemon flavor provides an interesting tang to the drink.

BEST OCCASION

TIME REQUIRED   2½ MINUTES

Prep: 2 min	Mix: 30sec

PROPORTIONS

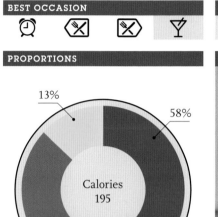

13%

58%

Calories
195

29%

FINISHED DRINK

INSTRUCTIONS

1 Pour vodka, coffee liqueur, and lemon juice into a rocks glass with ice cubes. **2** Stir well.
3 Garnish with a lemon wedge.

1	2	3

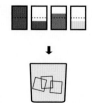

Black Russian

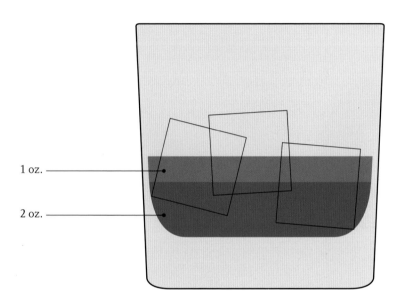

1 oz.

2 oz.

KEY

■ Vodka

■ Coffee Liqueur

DESCRIPTION

According to most drink historians, the Black Russian was first introduced in 1949 by Gustave Tops, a bartender at the Hotel Metropole in Brussels, Belgium, in honor of the U.S. ambassador to Luxembourg, Perle Mesta. The cocktail is named after its use of vodka, a stereotypical Russian spirit, and the darkness of the drink caused by the coffee liqueur. For something different, try adding cola.

BEST OCCASION				TIME REQUIRED	1½ MINUTES
⏰	⊠	⊠	🍸	Prep: 1 min	Mix: 30 sec

PROPORTIONS

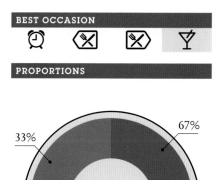

33%
67%

Calories
191

FINISHED DRINK

INSTRUCTIONS

1 Pour vodka and coffee liqueur into a rocks glass with ice cubes. **2** Stir well.

1	2

Bloody Mary

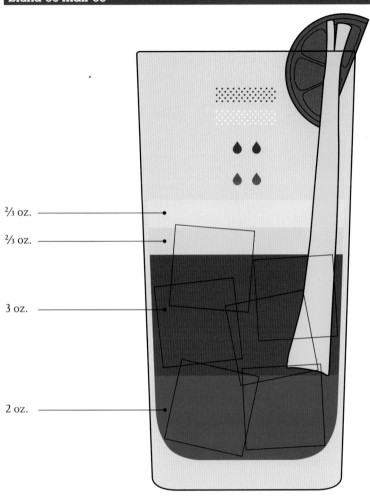

2/3 oz.

2/3 oz.

3 oz.

2 oz.

INGREDIENTS

KEY

- Vodka
- Tomato Juice
- Lemon Juice
- Horseradish Sauce
- Worcestershire Sauce
- Hot Sauce
- Salt & Pepper
- Celery Stalk
- Lime

DESCRIPTION

One of the most interesting ingredient combinations, the Bloody Mary is a cocktail meant for morning consumption, often used as a hangover cure. While the origin of the drink is disputed, most drink historians credit Fernand Petiot, a bartender at Harry's New York Bar in Paris, with the cocktail's creation in the 1920s. Try replacing vodka with tequila for a Bloody Maria.

BEST OCCASION

TIME REQUIRED   5 MINUTES

Prep: 3 min	Mix: 2 min

PROPORTIONS

FINISHED DRINK

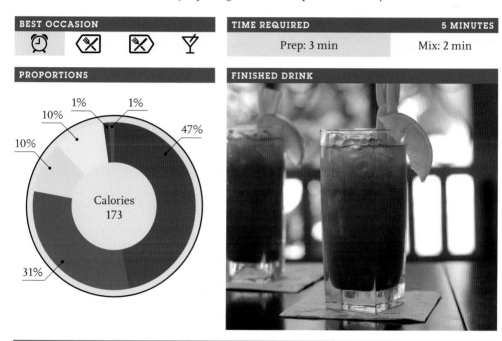

Calories
173

1%
1%
10%
47%
10%
31%

INSTRUCTIONS

1 Combine vodka, tomato juice, lemon juice, horseradish sauce, Worcestershire sauce, hot sauce, salt, and pepper in a cocktail shaker. **2** Shake with ice. **3** Empty the contents into a highball glass filled with ice. **4** Garnish with a lime wedge and celery stalk.

1	2	3	4

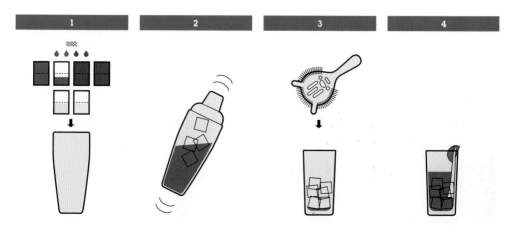

Blue Lagoon

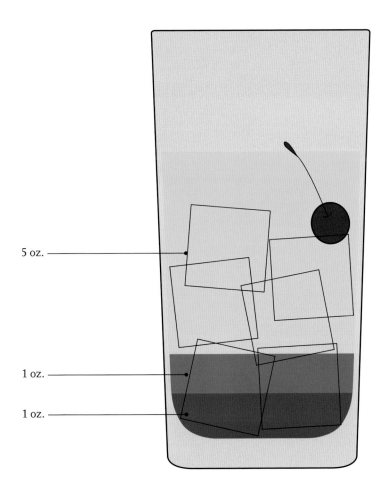

5 oz.

1 oz.

1 oz.

INGREDIENTS

KEY

- Vodka
- Blue Curaçao
- Lemonade
- Cherry

DESCRIPTION

Many attribute the creation of the Blue Lagoon to Andy MacElhone in 1972. MacElhone was the son of Harry of Harry's New York Bar in Paris, France, and supposedly invented the drink to showcase the vibrant blue hue of curaçao, a new liqueur at the time.

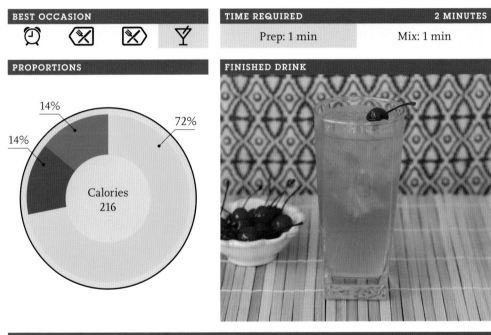

BEST OCCASION

TIME REQUIRED — 2 MINUTES

Prep: 1 min   Mix: 1 min

PROPORTIONS

14%
14%
72%

Calories
216

FINISHED DRINK

INSTRUCTIONS

1 Pour vodka and blue curaçao into a highball glass with ice cubes. **2** Fill with lemonade. **3** Stir well. **4** Garnish with a cherry.

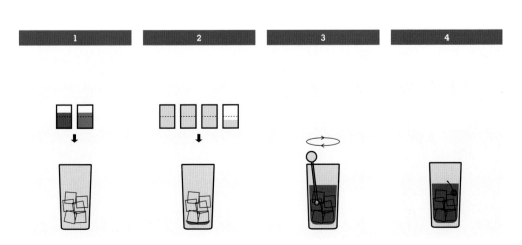

1   2   3   4

Cape Codder

keyp kod-er

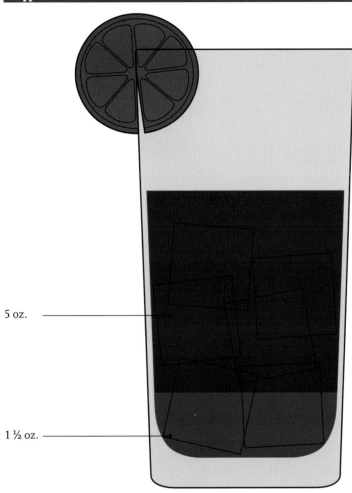

5 oz.

1 ½ oz.

INGREDIENTS

Vodka

Cranberry Juice

Lime

DESCRIPTION

Typically enjoyed as a summer cocktail, the Cape Codder was named after the coastal resort in Massachusetts. The drink was inspired by the abundance of cranberries found in the area.

BEST OCCASION

TIME REQUIRED — 1½ MINUTES

Prep: 1 min | Mix: 30 sec

PROPORTIONS

FINISHED DRINK

23%   77%

Calories
184

INSTRUCTIONS

1 Pour vodka and cranberry juice into a highball glass with ice cubes. **2** Stir well. **3** Garnish with a lime wheel.

1	2	3

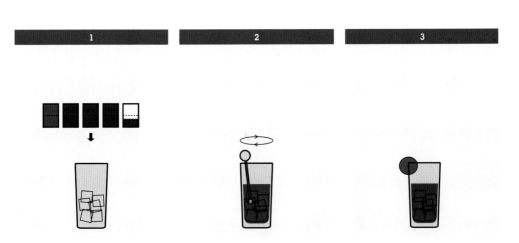

Cosmopolitan

koz-muh-pol-i-tn

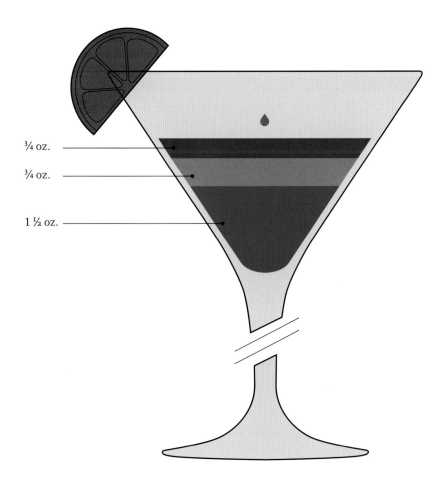

¾ oz.

¾ oz.

1 ½ oz.

INGREDIENTS

KEY

- Vodka
- Triple Sec
- Cranberry Juice
- Lime Juice
- Lime

DESCRIPTION

A fruity alternative to the Martini, the Cosmopolitan has become a wildly popular cocktail over the past decade, especially among women. The drink's origins are widely contested, with bartenders in Minneapolis, New York, San Francisco, South Beach, and Provincetown claiming its invention. If cranberry juice is excluded, the drink becomes a Kamikaze.

BEST OCCASION	TIME REQUIRED	3 MINUTES
	Prep: 2 min	Mix: 1 min

PROPORTIONS

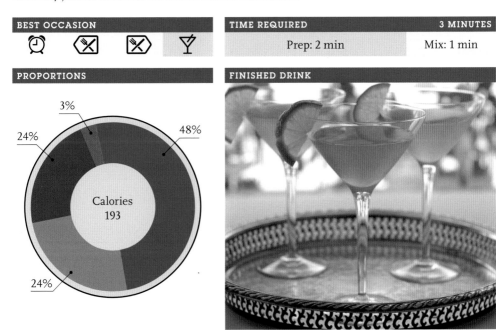

Calories
193

3%
24%
48%
24%

FINISHED DRINK

INSTRUCTIONS

1 Combine vodka, triple sec, cranberry juice, and a dash of lime juice in a cocktail shaker.
2 Shake with ice. **3** Strain into a chilled cocktail glass. **4** Garnish with a lime wedge.

1	2	3	4

Creamsicle

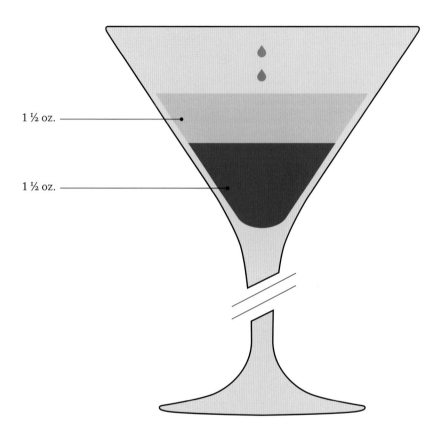

1 ½ oz.

1 ½ oz.

KEY

- Vanilla Vodka
- Orange Vodka
- Triple Sec
- Orange Juice

DESCRIPTION

The Creamsicle is the grown-up version of the favorite childhood frozen dessert. Try creating a Frozen Creamsicle by replacing orange juice with orange sherbet and combining with ice in a blender.

BEST OCCASION

TIME REQUIRED — **2 MINUTES**

| Prep: 1 min | Mix: 1 min |

PROPORTIONS

3% 3% 47%

Calories
218

47%

FINISHED DRINK

INSTRUCTIONS

1 Combine vanilla vodka, orange vodka, a dash of triple sec, and a dash of orange juice in a cocktail shaker. **2** Shake with ice. **3** Strain into a chilled cocktail glass.

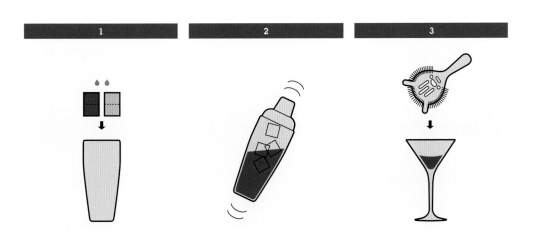

| 1 | 2 | 3 |

French Martini

¾ oz.

1 oz.

1 ½ oz.

INGREDIENTS

Vodka

Black Raspberry
Liqueur

Pineapple Juice

Lemon

DESCRIPTION

The French Martini is commonly made with Chambord, a French raspberry liqueur, giving the cocktail its name. The pineapple juice adds a tropical element. Try replacing vodka with gin for a common variation.

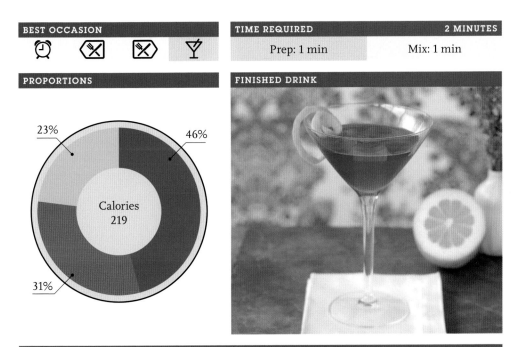

BEST OCCASION

TIME REQUIRED   2 MINUTES

Prep: 1 min   Mix: 1 min

PROPORTIONS

23%
46%
Calories
219
31%

FINISHED DRINK

INSTRUCTIONS

1 Combine vodka, black raspberry liqueur, and pineapple juice in a cocktail shaker. **2** Shake with ice. **3** Strain into a chilled cocktail glass. **4** Garnish with a lemon twist.

| 1 | 2 | 3 | 4 |

Godmother

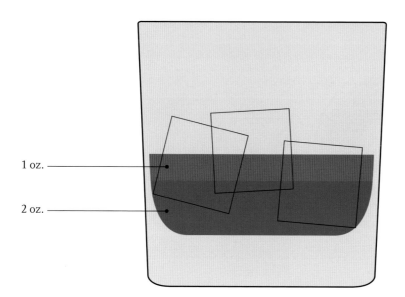

1 oz. ————

2 oz. ————

INGREDIENTS

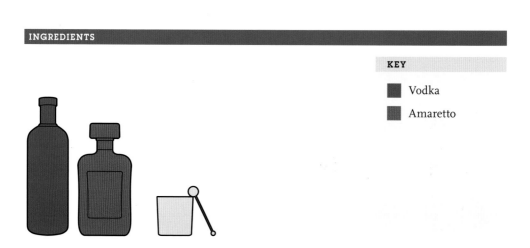

KEY

■ Vodka
■ Amaretto

159

DESCRIPTION

The Godmother is a simple, smooth duo cocktail combining vodka and amaretto. Replacing vodka with whiskey makes a Godfather. Mixing the drink with Cognac instead of vodka creates a Godchild.

BEST OCCASION

TIME REQUIRED
1½ MINUTES
Prep: 1 min | Mix: 30 sec

PROPORTIONS

33%
67%

Calories
248

FINISHED DRINK

INSTRUCTIONS

1 Pour vodka and amaretto into a rocks glass with ice cubes. **2** Stir well.

1

2

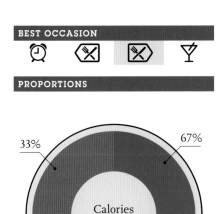

Greyhound

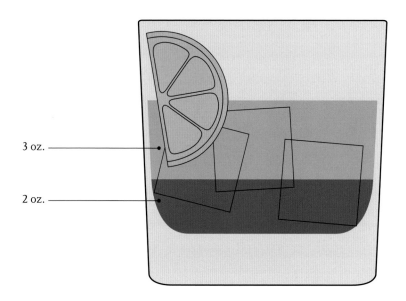

3 oz. ————

2 oz. ————

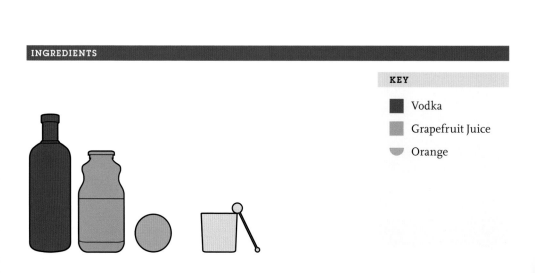

KEY

■ Vodka

■ Grapefruit Juice

◗ Orange

DESCRIPTION

The Greyhound is a different take on the Screwdriver, with the orange juice replaced with grapefruit juice. Use white grapefruit juice, replace vodka with gin, and salt the glass rim to make a Salty Dog.

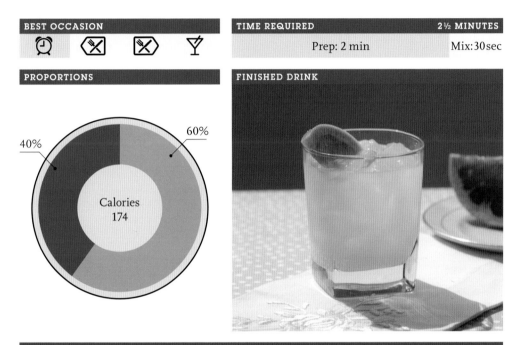

BEST OCCASION

TIME REQUIRED   2½ MINUTES

Prep: 2 min   Mix: 30 sec

PROPORTIONS

FINISHED DRINK

40%

60%

Calories
174

INSTRUCTIONS

1 Pour vodka and grapefruit juice into a rocks glass with ice cubes. **2** Stir well. **3** Garnish with an orange wedge.

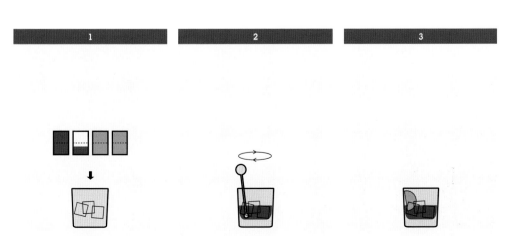

1   2   3

Harvey Wallbanger

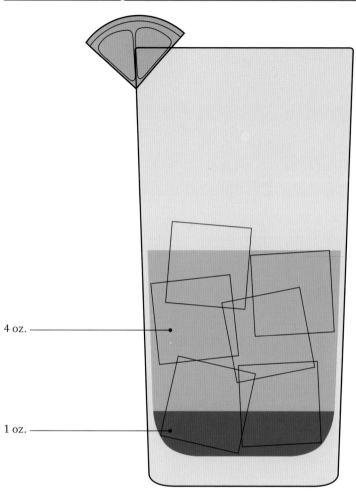

4 oz.

1 oz.

INGREDIENTS

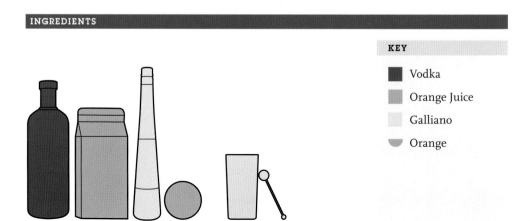

KEY

- Vodka
- Orange Juice
- Galliano
- Orange

DESCRIPTION

According to cocktail lore, the Harvey Wallbanger was named after a surfer named Harvey in Manhattan Beach, California, in the 1960s. Harvey consumed too many of the drinks one night and was seen the next morning banging his head, complaining of a massive hangover.

BEST OCCASION

TIME REQUIRED — 2½ MINUTES

Prep: 2 min   Mix: 30 sec

PROPORTIONS

2%
19%
79%

Calories
133

FINISHED DRINK

INSTRUCTIONS

1 Pour vodka and orange juice into a highball glass with ice cubes. **2** Stir well. **3** Float Galliano on top. **4** Garnish with an orange wedge.

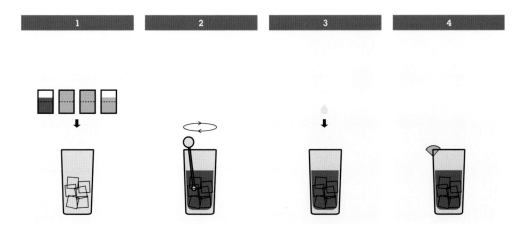

Kamikaze

kah-mi-kah-zee

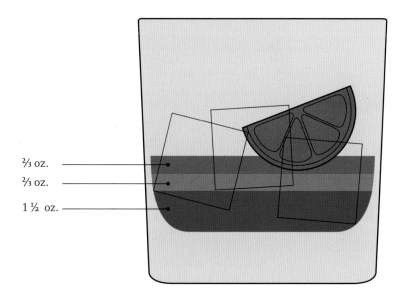

2/3 oz.
2/3 oz.
1 1/2 oz.

INGREDIENTS

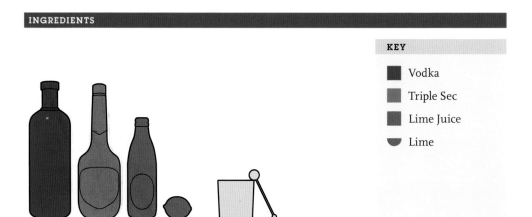

KEY

■ Vodka
■ Triple Sec
■ Lime Juice
▬ Lime

DESCRIPTION

Some people jokingly speculate that the Kamikaze name comes from its ingredients: vodka, triple sec, and lime juice—or VTL, standing for Very Tragic Landing. The addition of cranberry juice creates a Cosmopolitan. Replace vodka with Southern Comfort for a SoCo Kamikaze.

BEST OCCASION

TIME REQUIRED   2½ MINUTES

Prep: 2 min	Mix: 30 sec

PROPORTIONS

24%

52%

Calories
178

24%

FINISHED DRINK

INSTRUCTIONS

1 Pour vodka, triple sec, and lime juice into a rocks glass with ice cubes. **2** Stir well. **3** Garnish with a lime wedge.

1	2	3

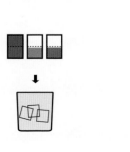

Lemon Drop

¾ oz.

¾ oz.

1 ½ oz.

INGREDIENTS

DESCRIPTION

The Lemon Drop is a great after-dinner drink and also makes for a popular shooter at parties. Try adding sugar to the glass rim for an extra touch of sweetness.

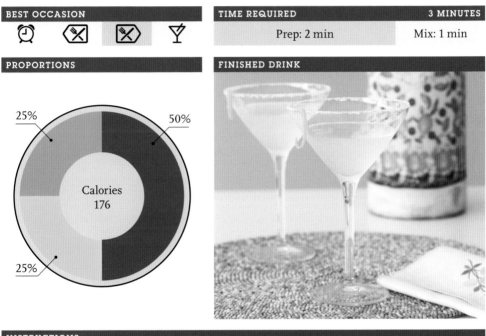

BEST OCCASION

TIME REQUIRED — 3 MINUTES

Prep: 2 min | Mix: 1 min

PROPORTIONS

25% | 50% | 25%

Calories 176

FINISHED DRINK

INSTRUCTIONS

1 Pour vodka, lemon juice, and simple syrup into a cocktail shaker. **2** Shake with ice. **3** Strain into a chilled cocktail glass. **4** Garnish with a lemon twist.

Long Island Iced Tea

lawng ahy-luhnd ahyst tee

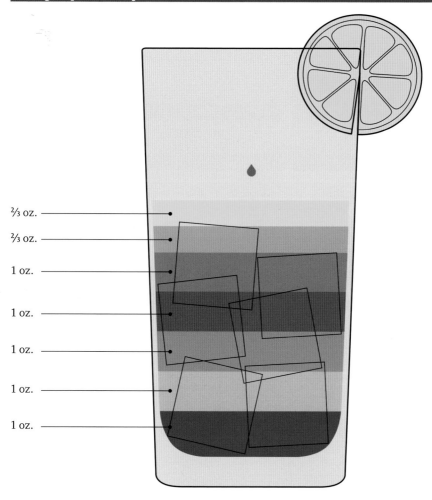

⅔ oz. ————
⅔ oz. ————
1 oz. ————
1 oz. ————
1 oz. ————
1 oz. ————
1 oz. ————

INGREDIENTS

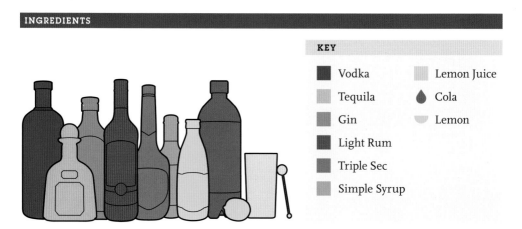

KEY

■	Vodka	▨	Lemon Juice
▨	Tequila	●	Cola
▨	Gin	▨	Lemon
■	Light Rum		
▨	Triple Sec		
▨	Simple Syrup		

DESCRIPTION

Who predicted the combination of five seemingly unrelated spirits would create such a tasty masterpiece? While there are many stories surrounding its creation, the most repeated one credits Robert "Rosebud" Butt from the Oak Beach Inn in Long Island, New York. The splash of cola gives the cocktail its iced tea appearance.

BEST OCCASION

TIME REQUIRED   5 MINUTES

Prep: 3 min   Mix: 2 min

PROPORTIONS

FINISHED DRINK

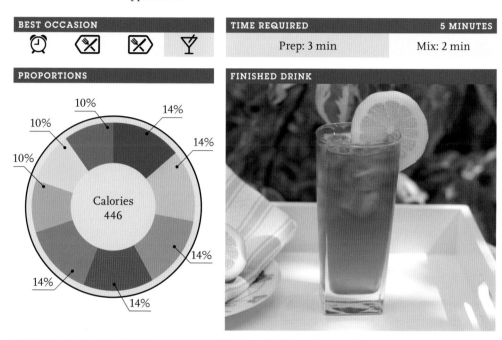

Calories 446

10% 10% 10% 14% 14% 14% 14% 14% 14%

INSTRUCTIONS

1 Pour vodka, tequila, gin, light rum, triple sec, simple syrup, and lemon juice into a highball glass with ice. **2** Stir well. **3** Add a dash of cola on top. **4** Garnish with a lemon wheel.

| 1 | 2 | 3 | 4 |

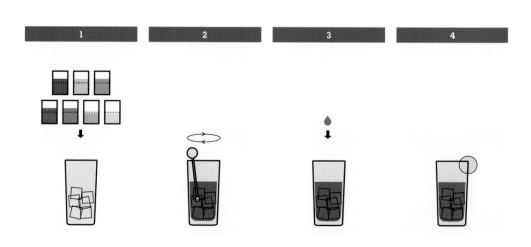

Madras

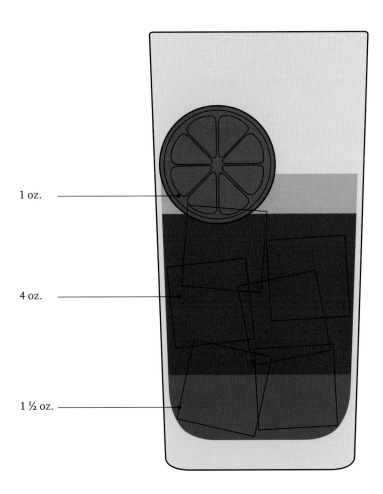

1 oz.

4 oz.

1 ½ oz.

INGREDIENTS

KEY

- Vodka
- Cranberry Juice
- Orange Juice
- Lime

DESCRIPTION

The Madras is a refreshing cocktail that is close in relation to the Sea Breeze and the Cape Codder due to the cranberry-vodka combination.

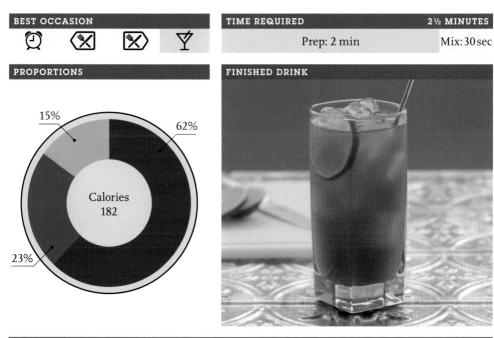

BEST OCCASION	TIME REQUIRED	2½ MINUTES
	Prep: 2 min	Mix: 30 sec

PROPORTIONS

15%
62%
23%

Calories
182

FINISHED DRINK

INSTRUCTIONS

1 Pour vodka, cranberry juice, and orange juice into a highball glass with ice. **2** Stir well.
3 Garnish with a lime wheel.

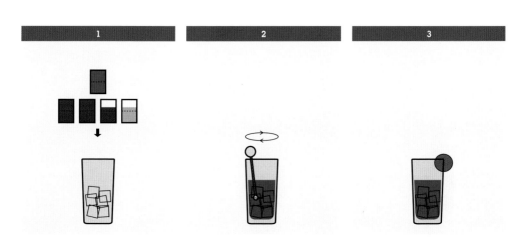

1	2	3

Moscow Mule

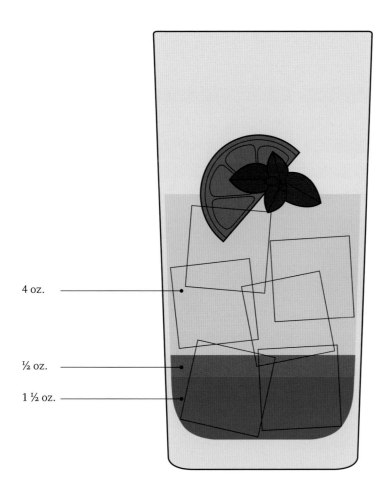

4 oz.

½ oz.

1 ½ oz.

INGREDIENTS

KEY

- Vodka
- Lime Juice
- Ginger Beer
- Lime
- Mint Sprig

DESCRIPTION

Legend has it the Moscow Mule was created in the 1940s by John G. Martin, a spirits distributor, who purchased the American rights to a new Russian vodka, called Smirnoff. While selling his spirit on the West Coast, Martin met Jack Morgan, owner of the Cock 'n Bull restaurant, who had an overstock of ginger beer. Martin combined Smirnoff with the ginger beer to create the Moscow Mule.

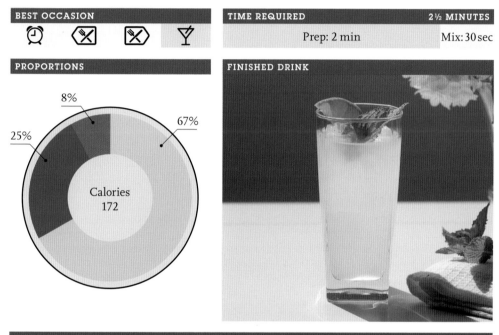

BEST OCCASION

TIME REQUIRED — 2½ MINUTES
Prep: 2 min Mix: 30 sec

PROPORTIONS

8%
67%
25%
Calories 172

FINISHED DRINK

INSTRUCTIONS

1 Pour vodka and lime juice into a highball glass with ice. **2** Top with ginger beer. **3** Garnish with a lime wedge and mint sprig.

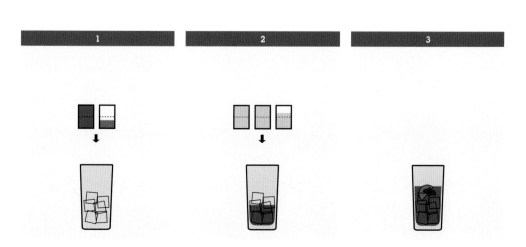

1 2 3

Mudslide

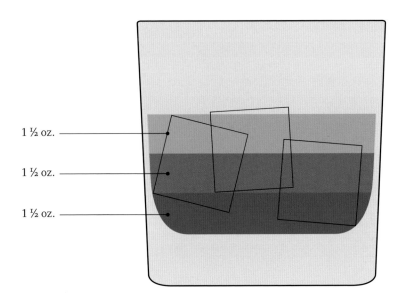

1 ½ oz.

1 ½ oz.

1 ½ oz.

KEY

■ Vodka

■ Coffee Liqueur

■ Irish Cream Liqueur

DESCRIPTION

The Mudslide is a popular dessert drink that is close in relation to the Black Russian. Try creating a Frozen Mudslide by blending the ingredients with a few scoops of vanilla ice cream and crushed ice—drizzle chocolate syrup on the inside of the glass before pouring in the blended contents.

BEST OCCASION

TIME REQUIRED   2 MINUTES

Prep: 1 min   Mix: 1 min

PROPORTIONS

FINISHED DRINK

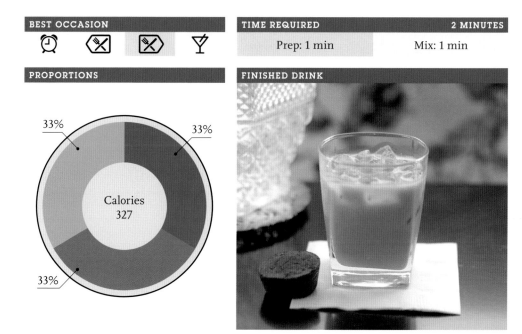

33%   33%   33%

Calories
327

INSTRUCTIONS

1 Combine vodka, coffee liqueur, and Irish cream liqueur in a cocktail shaker. **2** Shake with ice. **3** Strain into a rocks glass with ice.

1	2	3

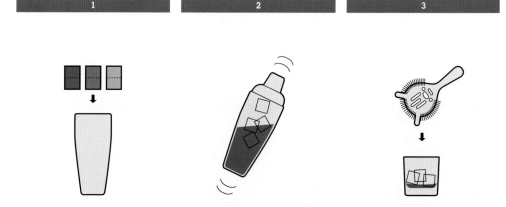

Screwdriver

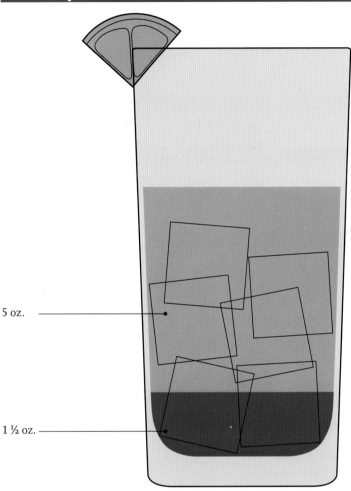

5 oz.

1 ½ oz.

INGREDIENTS

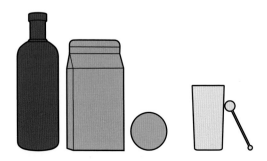

KEY

■ Vodka
■ Orange Juice
■ Orange

DESCRIPTION

A simple cocktail perfect with breakfast or brunch, the Screwdriver is thought to have been created in the 1950s when a group of U.S. engineers were working in a hot desert in the Middle East. The engineers added orange juice to their vodka and stirred the drink with a screwdriver, the nearest available tool.

BEST OCCASION

TIME REQUIRED   2½ MINUTES

Prep: 2 min   Mix: 30 sec

PROPORTIONS

FINISHED DRINK

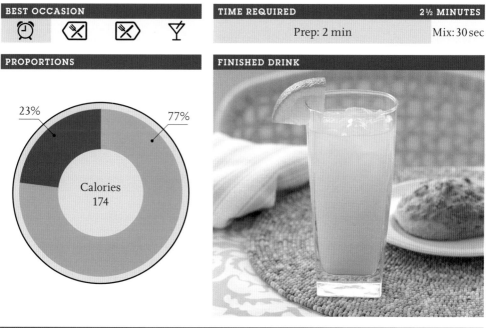

23%

77%

Calories
174

INSTRUCTIONS

1 Pour vodka and orange juice into a highball glass with ice. **2** Stir well. **3** Garnish with an orange wedge.

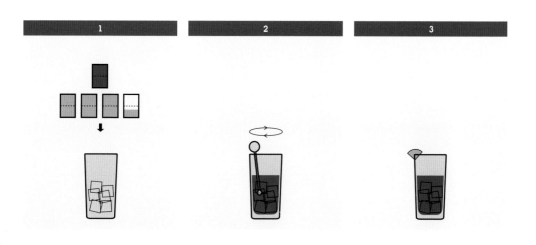

Sea Breeze

see breez

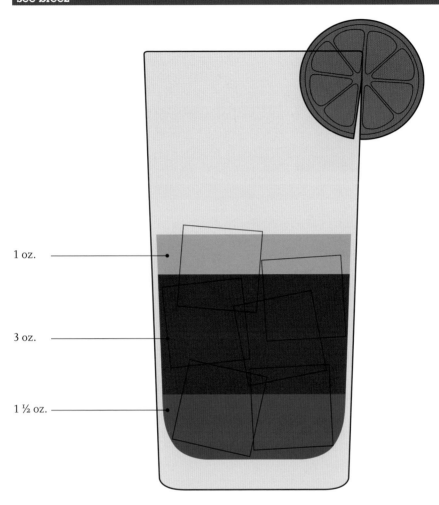

1 oz.

3 oz.

1 ½ oz.

INGREDIENTS

DESCRIPTION

The Sea Breeze is essentially a Cape Codder with grapefruit juice added. The cocktail is thought to have been created in the late 1920s but originally included gin and grenadine.

BEST OCCASION

TIME REQUIRED   2½ MINUTES

Prep: 2 min   Mix: 30 sec

PROPORTIONS

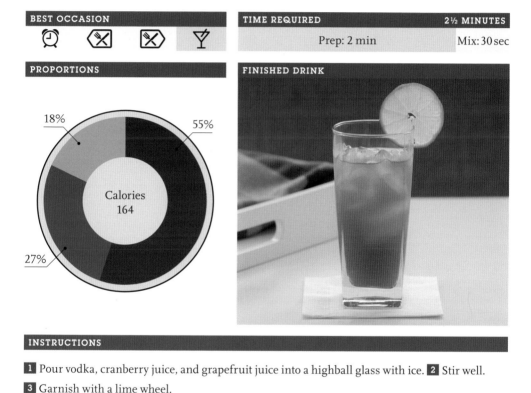

18%

55%

Calories
164

27%

FINISHED DRINK

INSTRUCTIONS

1 Pour vodka, cranberry juice, and grapefruit juice into a highball glass with ice. **2** Stir well. **3** Garnish with a lime wheel.

| 1 | 2 | 3 |

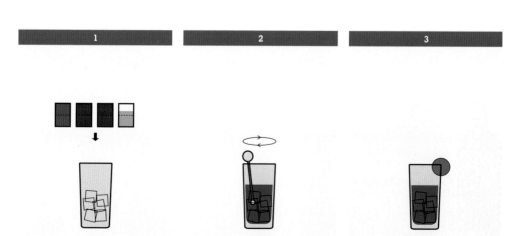

Sex on the Beach

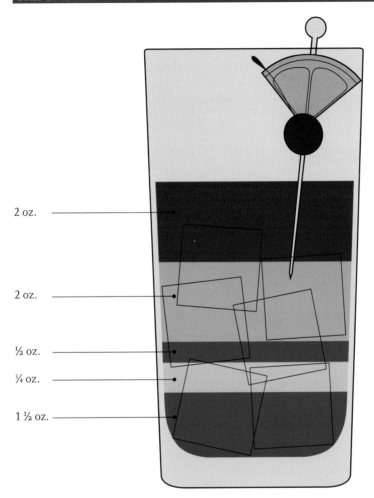

2 oz.

2 oz.

½ oz.

¾ oz.

1 ½ oz.

INGREDIENTS

KEY

- Vodka
- Peach Schnapps
- Crème de Cassis
- Orange Juice
- Cranberry Juice
- Orange
- Cherry

DESCRIPTION

Especially popular in the 1980s, Sex on the Beach is a big crowd pleaser packed with fruity taste. Try adding a dash of grenadine for extra flavor.

BEST OCCASION

TIME REQUIRED   **3 MINUTES**

Prep: 2 min   Mix: 1 min

PROPORTIONS

7%
11%
30%
Calories
258
22%
30%

FINISHED DRINK

INSTRUCTIONS

1 Combine vodka, peach schnapps, crème de cassis, orange juice, and cranberry juice in a cocktail shaker. **2** Shake with ice. **3** Strain into a highball glass with ice. **4** Garnish with an orange wedge and cherry.

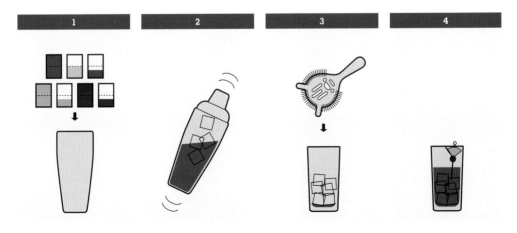

| 1 | 2 | 3 | 4 |

White Russian

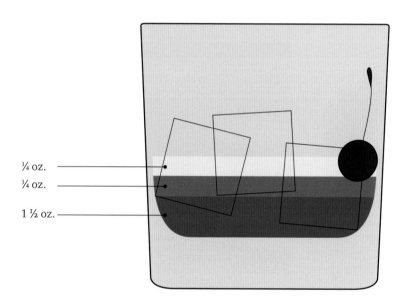

¾ oz. ⎯⎯⎯⎯⎯⎯

¾ oz. ⎯⎯⎯⎯⎯⎯

1 ½ oz. ⎯⎯⎯⎯⎯

INGREDIENTS

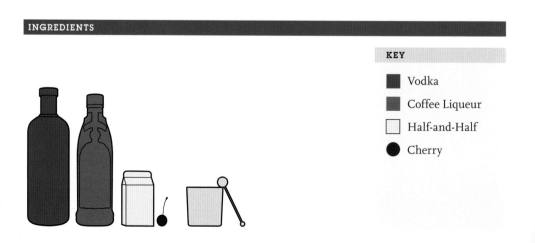

KEY

■ Vodka
■ Coffee Liqueur
□ Half-and-Half
● Cherry

DESCRIPTION

The White Russian is a popular dessert drink that dates to the 1960s or earlier. The cocktail gets its name from two of its primary ingredients—vodka and cream.

BEST OCCASION

TIME REQUIRED
1½ MINUTES
| Prep: 1 min | Mix: 30 sec |

PROPORTIONS

25%
50%
Calories
173
25%

FINISHED DRINK

INSTRUCTIONS

1 Pour vodka, coffee liqueur, and half-and-half into a rocks glass with ice cubes. **2** Stir well. **3** Garnish with a cherry (optional).

| 1 | 2 | 3 |

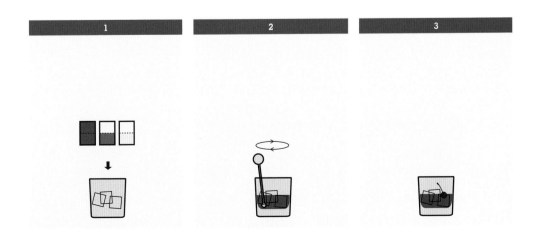

Whiskey

Algonquin

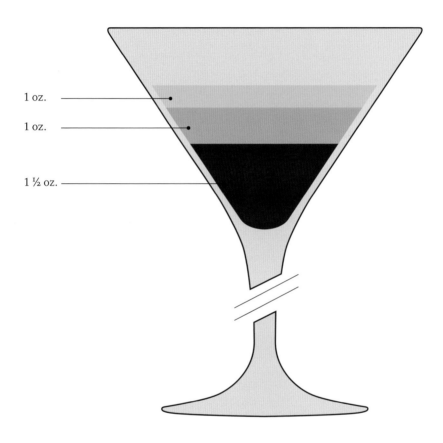

1 oz.

1 oz.

1 ½ oz.

INGREDIENTS

KEY

■ Whiskey (Rye)

■ Dry vermouth

■ Pineapple Juice

DESCRIPTION

The Algonquin is named after the famed Algonquin Hotel in New York City. During the 1920s, the hotel was a popular gathering place for the Round Table, the group of luminaries including Dorothy Parker who met to discuss various topics of the day. The Algonquin cocktail is well balanced with fruit and whiskey and is said to have inspired the New Yorker.

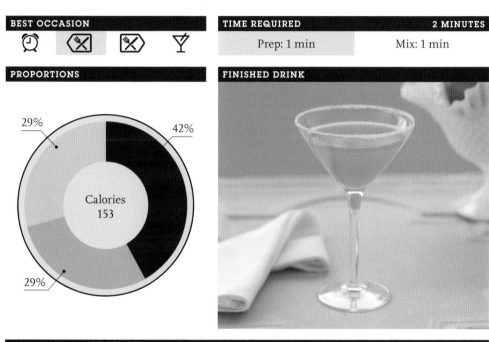

BEST OCCASION

TIME REQUIRED — 2 MINUTES
Prep: 1 min   Mix: 1 min

PROPORTIONS

29%
42%
Calories
153
29%

FINISHED DRINK

INSTRUCTIONS

1 Pour whiskey, dry vermouth, and pineapple juice in a cocktail shaker. **2** Shake with ice.
3 Strain into a chilled cocktail glass.

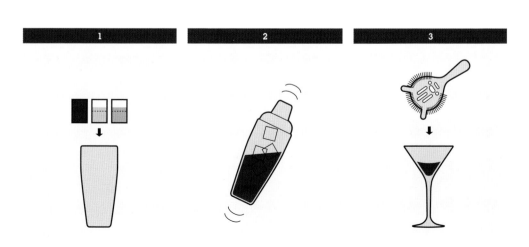

1   2   3

Godfather

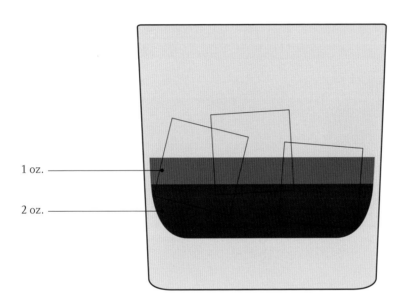

1 oz.

2 oz.

INGREDIENTS

KEY

■ Whisky (Scotch)
■ Amaretto

DESCRIPTION

Said to have been inspired by Francis Ford Coppola's *Godfather* trilogy, this cocktail combines sweet Italian liqueur, amaretto, with the complex and hard flavors of Scotch. A softer alternative to the Godfather, the Godmother uses vodka instead of Scotch.

BEST OCCASION

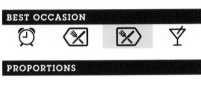

TIME REQUIRED — 1½ MINUTES

Prep: 1 min | Mix: 30 sec

PROPORTIONS

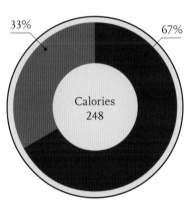

33%   67%

Calories
248

FINISHED DRINK

INSTRUCTIONS

1 Pour Scotch whisky and amaretto into a rocks glass with ice cubes. **2** Stir well.

1	2

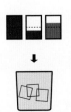

Highball

hahy-bawl

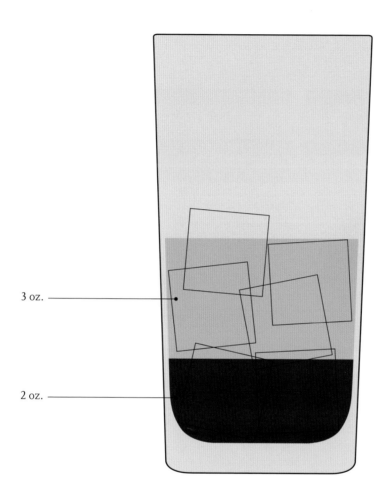

3 oz.

2 oz.

INGREDIENTS

DESCRIPTION

Refreshing and simple, the Highball is a great entry-level drink for those developing a palate for whiskey. A Big Ginger is a Highball made with Irish whiskey and fresh squeezed lemon and lime.

BEST OCCASION

TIME REQUIRED   1½ MINUTES

Prep: 1 min	Mix: 30 sec

PROPORTIONS

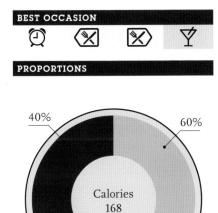

40%   60%

Calories
168

FINISHED DRINK

INSTRUCTIONS

1 Fill a highball glass with ice cubes. **2** Pour whiskey and ginger ale into the glass.

1	2

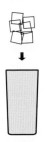

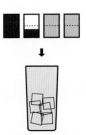

Hot Toddy

hot tod-ee

1 oz.

1 oz.

6 oz.

INGREDIENTS

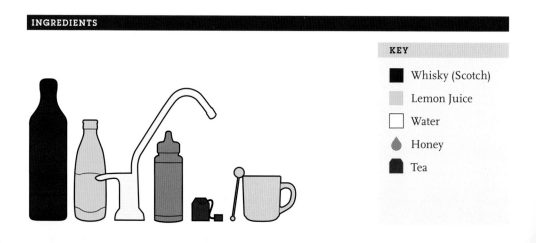

KEY

- Whisky (Scotch)
- Lemon Juice
- Water
- Honey
- Tea

DESCRIPTION

A classic warm whisky drink, the Hot Toddy is best enjoyed in the morning, when it's chilly outside, or when recovering from a nagging cold or sore throat. Try substituting Scotch with rum, brandy, or other whiskeys.

BEST OCCASION

TIME REQUIRED   4 MINUTES

Prep: 1 min   Mix: 3 min

PROPORTIONS

FINISHED DRINK

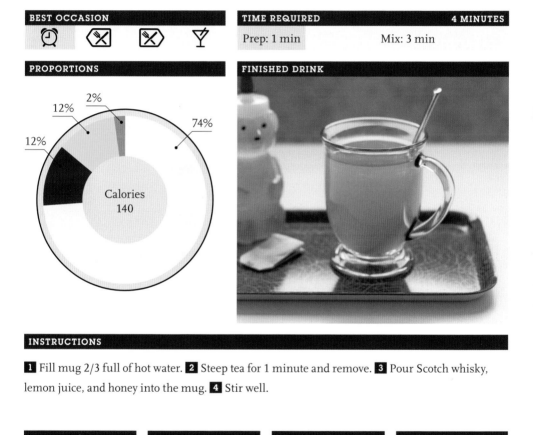

2%
12%
12%
74%

Calories
140

INSTRUCTIONS

1 Fill mug 2/3 full of hot water. **2** Steep tea for 1 minute and remove. **3** Pour Scotch whisky, lemon juice, and honey into the mug. **4** Stir well.

| 1 | 2 | 3 | 4 |

Irish Coffee

ahy-rish kaw-fee

~2 oz.

2 oz.

5 oz.

INGREDIENTS

KEY

- Whiskey (Irish)
- Coffee
- Whipped Cream
- Brown Sugar

DESCRIPTION

During a gloomy winter day in the 1940s, as legend has it, a group of Americans in Shannon, Ireland, were waiting to disembark on a seaplane. The head chef at the terminal decided to add whiskey to the passengers' coffee to warm them. Amused, the passengers thought they were being served Brazilian coffee—the chef responded, telling them it was Irish coffee.

BEST OCCASION

TIME REQUIRED   10 MINUTES

Prep: 9 min   Mix: 1 min—•

PROPORTIONS

FINISHED DRINK

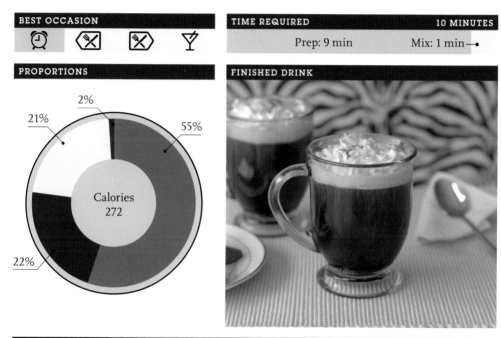

2%
21%
55%
Calories
272
22%

INSTRUCTIONS

1 Pour coffee, Irish whiskey, and brown sugar into a mug. **2** Stir well. **3** Top with whipped cream.

Manhattan

man-hat-n

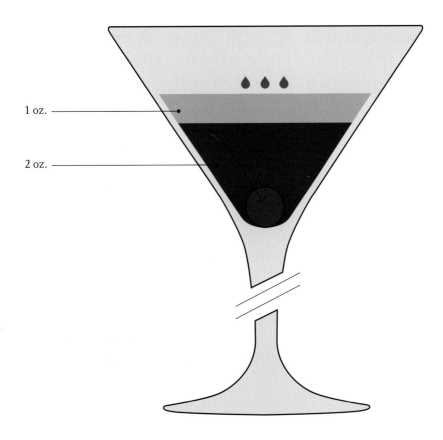

1 oz.

2 oz.

INGREDIENTS

KEY

■ Whiskey (Bourbon)

■ Sweet Vermouth

● Angostura Bitters

● Cherry

DESCRIPTION

A popular but questionable account has it that Winston Churchill's mother invented this drink at a banquet held at the Manhattan Club in New York City in honor of Samuel J. Tilden, a U.S. presidential candidate. Quickly gaining popularity, the drink soon became known by the name of the club where it originated—or so the story goes. A Rob Roy is a Manhattan made with Scotch whisky.

BEST OCCASION

TIME REQUIRED 2 MINUTES

Prep: 1 min   Mix: 1 min

PROPORTIONS

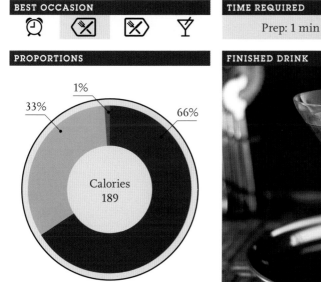

1%
33%
66%
Calories
189

FINISHED DRINK

INSTRUCTIONS

1 Pour whiskey, sweet vermouth, and Angostura bitters (3 dashes) into a shaker. **2** Shake with ice. **3** Strain into a chilled cocktail glass. **4** Garnish with a cherry.

1   2   3   4

Mint Julep

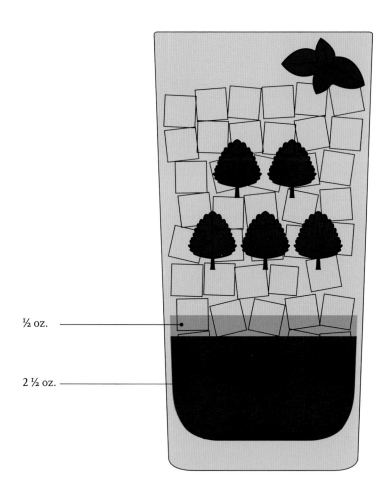

½ oz.

2 ½ oz.

INGREDIENTS

KEY

- Whiskey (Bourbon)
- Simple Syrup
- Mint Leaves

DESCRIPTION

The Mint Julep is well known as the official cocktail of the Kentucky Derby. Each year, an estimated 120,000 Mint Juleps are served at the Churchill Downs horse track over the two-day Kentucky Oaks and Kentucky Derby races.

BEST OCCASION

TIME REQUIRED   3 MINUTES

Prep: 1 min   Mix: 2 min

PROPORTIONS

FINISHED DRINK

17%

83%

Calories
218

INSTRUCTIONS

1 Combine simple syrup and 5 mint leaves in a highball glass. **2** Muddle well. **3** Pour in whiskey. **4** Fill with crushed ice and stir. **5** Garnish with mint sprig.

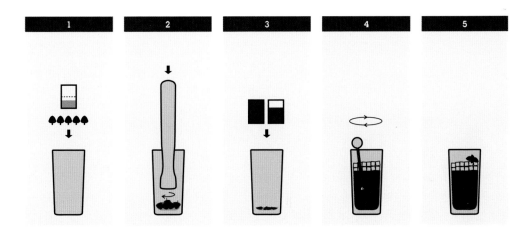

New Yorker

1 tsp.
½ oz.
1 oz.

2 oz.

INGREDIENTS

KEY

- Whisky (Canadian)
- Lime Juice
- Simple Syrup
- Grenadine
- Lemon

DESCRIPTION

The New Yorker is a smooth, sweet drink that pairs well with chocolate and other desserts. This drink is best enjoyed with a quality Canadian whisky. The Algonquin cocktail is said to have inspired the New Yorker.

BEST OCCASION

TIME REQUIRED   3 MINUTES

Prep: 2 min   Mix: 1 min

PROPORTIONS

5%
14%
54%
Calories
204
27%

FINISHED DRINK

INSTRUCTIONS

1 Pour whisky, lime juice, simple syrup, and grenadine into a shaker. **2** Shake with ice.
3 Strain into a chilled cocktail glass. **4** Garnish with lemon twist.

| 1 | 2 | 3 | 4 |

Old Fashioned

ohld fash-uhnd

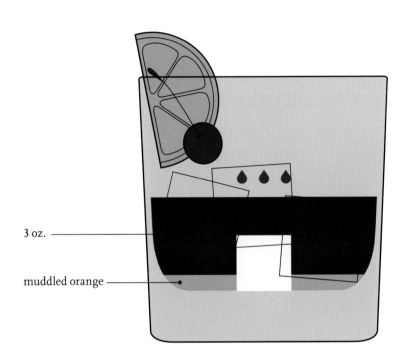

3 oz.

muddled orange

INGREDIENTS

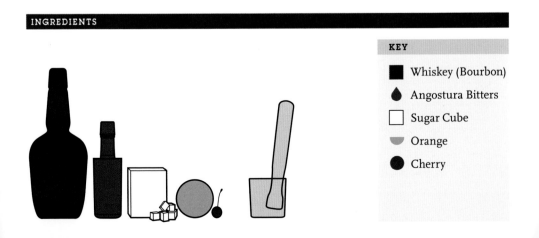

KEY

- Whiskey (Bourbon)
- Angostura Bitters
- Sugar Cube
- Orange
- Cherry

DESCRIPTION

The Old Fashioned is truly a classic cocktail. A popular story attributes the drink's creation to a bartender around 1900 at the Pendennis Club in Louisville, Kentucky. The drink was supposedly popularized by a local bourbon distiller, Colonel James E. Pepper, who later introduced the cocktail to the Waldorf-Astoria Hotel in New York City.

BEST OCCASION

TIME REQUIRED   4 MINUTES

Prep: 2 min   Mix: 2 min

PROPORTIONS

FINISHED DRINK

2%
5%
7%
86%

Calories
233

INSTRUCTIONS

1 Place sugar cube, Angostura bitters (3 dashes), and orange slice in a rocks glass. **2** Muddle until sugar dissolves. **3** Add ice and whiskey. **4** Garnish with an orange wedge and cherry.

1	2	3	4

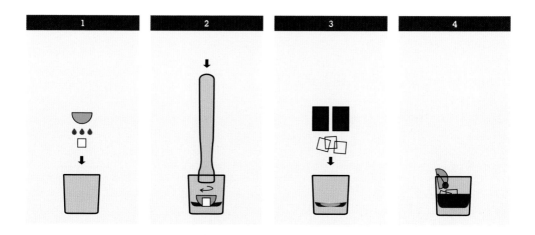

Rusty Nail

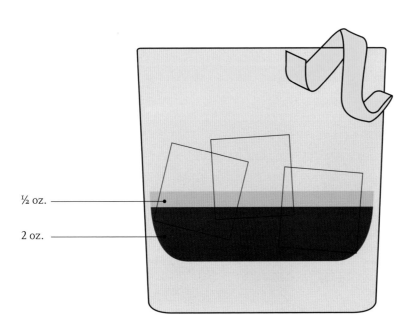

½ oz.

2 oz.

INGREDIENTS

KEY

■ Whisky (Scotch)

▨ Drambuie

▨ Lemon

DESCRIPTION

The Rusty Nail is a quick duo cocktail that is sure to relax—balanced and pleasing to Scotch and non-Scotch drinkers alike due to the honey and herbal hints of the Drambuie.

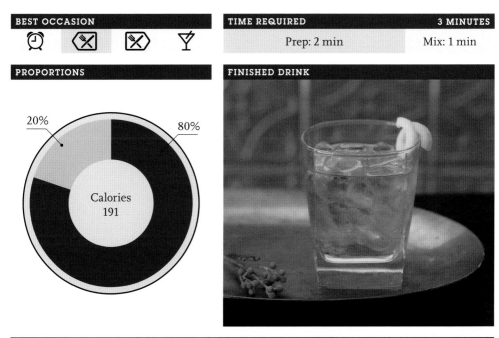

BEST OCCASION

TIME REQUIRED · 3 MINUTES

| Prep: 2 min | Mix: 1 min |

PROPORTIONS

20%
80%

Calories
191

FINISHED DRINK

INSTRUCTIONS

1 Pour Scotch whisky and Drambuie into a rocks glass with ice. **2** Stir well. **3** Garnish with a lemon twist.

| 1 | 2 | 3 |

Sazerac

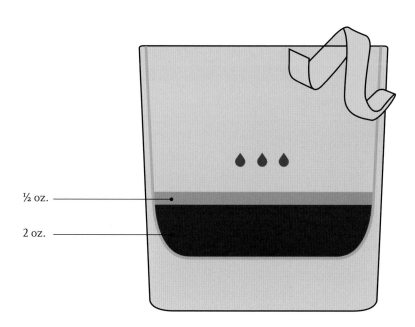

½ oz.

2 oz.

KEY

- Whiskey (Rye)
- Simple Syrup
- Peychaud's Bitters
- Pernod (Absinthe)
- Lemon

DESCRIPTION

In 1959, the Sazerac was the signature drink of the Sazerac Coffee House in New Orleans, where it received its name. The cocktail is enhanced by the licorice-flavored Pernod swirled in the glass before the other ingredients are added.

BEST OCCASION	TIME REQUIRED	4 MINUTES
	Prep: 2 min	Mix: 2 min

PROPORTIONS

72%
18%
6%
4%

Calories
207

FINISHED DRINK

INSTRUCTIONS

1 Rinse a chilled rocks glass with Pernod. **2** Pour whiskey, simple syrup, and Peychaud's bitters (3 dashes) into a shaker. **3** Shake with ice. **4** Strain into the glass. **5** Garnish with a lemon twist.

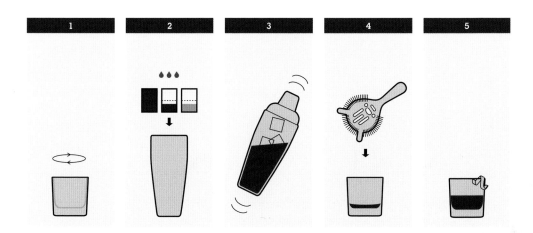

1	2	3	4	5

Waldorf

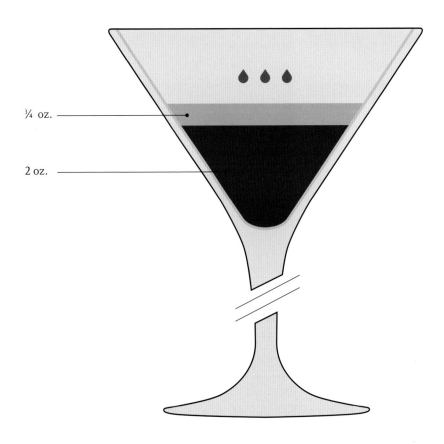

¾ oz.

2 oz.

INGREDIENTS

KEY

- ■ Whiskey (Rye)
- ■ Sweet Vermouth
- ▦ Pernod (Absinthe)
- ● Angostura Bitters

DESCRIPTION

Known as one of the original signature cocktails of the Waldorf-Astoria bar in New York City, the Waldorf is a unique whiskey-based drink that creatively blends the licorice taste of Pernod.

BEST OCCASION

TIME REQUIRED   2 MINUTES

Prep: 1 min	Mix: 1 min

PROPORTIONS

FINISHED DRINK

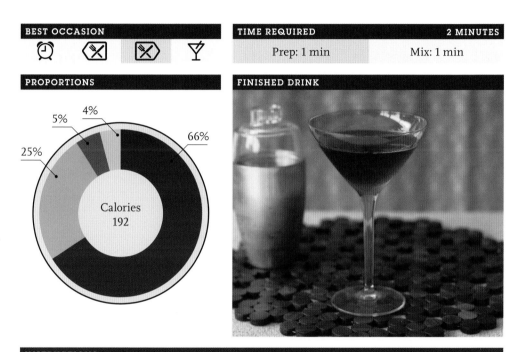

4%
5%
66%
25%

Calories
192

INSTRUCTIONS

1 Rinse a chilled cocktail glass with Pernod. **2** Pour whiskey, sweet vermouth, and Angostura bitters (3 dashes) into a shaker. **3** Shake with ice. **4** Strain into the glass.

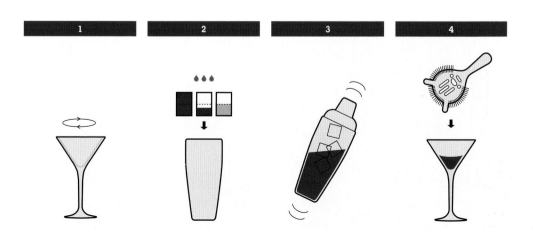

1	2	3	4

Whiskey Sour

hwis-kee sou-er

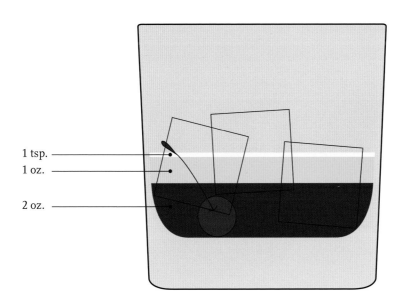

1 tsp. —

1 oz. —

2 oz. —

KEY

■ Whiskey (Rye)

▨ Lemon Juice

☐ Superfine Sugar

● Cherry

DESCRIPTION

One of the most popular sour drinks, the Whiskey Sour is a tart, yet surprisingly sweet and fresh cocktail. The Whiskey Sour is great as an after-dinner drink or for a hot summer afternoon.

BEST OCCASION

TIME REQUIRED   2 MINUTES

| Prep: 1 min | Mix: 1 min |

PROPORTIONS

FINISHED DRINK

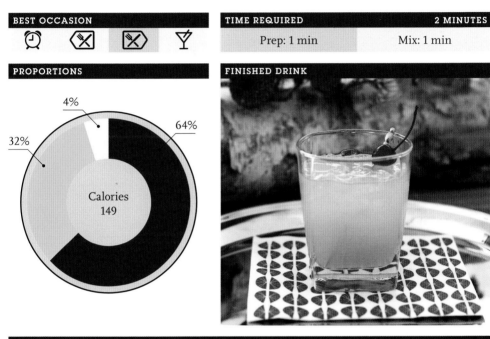

4%
64%
32%

Calories
149

INSTRUCTIONS

1 Pour whiskey, lemon juice, and superfine sugar into a cocktail shaker. **2** Shake with ice.
3 Strain into a chilled rocks glass. **4** Garnish with a cherry.

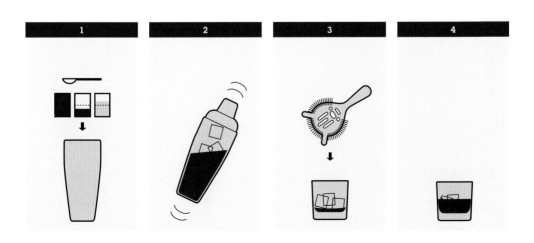

| 1 | 2 | 3 | 4 |

Liqueurs

Amaretto Sour

Blackjack

Ferrari

French Connection

Fuzzy Navel

Golden Cadillac

Grasshopper

Toasted Almond

Amaretto Sour

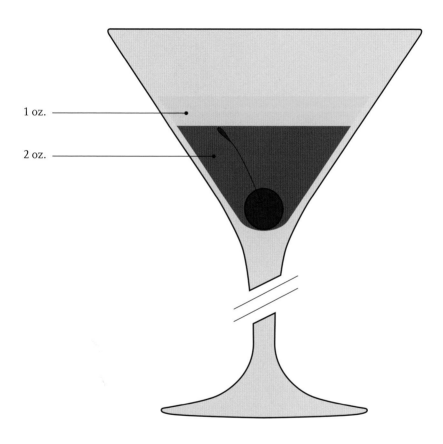

1 oz.

2 oz.

INGREDIENTS

KEY

- Amaretto
- Lemon Juice
- ● Cherry

DESCRIPTION

Quite possibly the most popular cocktail to use amaretto, the Amaretto Sour likely originated in Italy. According to popular amaretto brand Disaronno, amaretto, made from almonds and apricots, is said to have been concocted by the young widowed model used by Italian artist Bernardino Luini to paint the Madonna in the Adoration fresco in the Santa Maria delle Grazie sanctuary in Saronno, Italy.

BEST OCCASION

TIME REQUIRED   2 MINUTES

Prep: 1 min | Mix: 1 min

PROPORTIONS

FINISHED DRINK

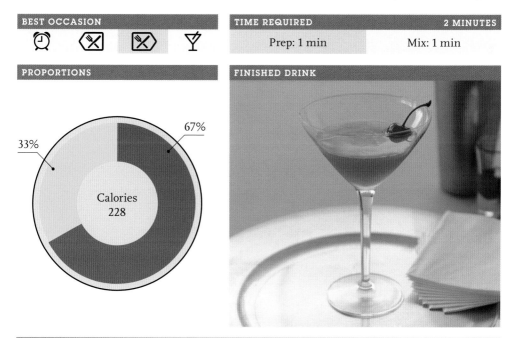

67%

33%

Calories
228

INSTRUCTIONS

1 Combine amaretto and lemon juice in a shaker. **2** Shake with ice. **3** Strain into a chilled cocktail glass. **4** Garnish with a cherry.

| 1 | 2 | 3 | 4 |

Blackjack

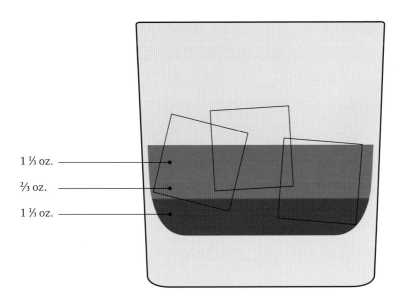

1 ⅓ oz.

⅔ oz.

1 ⅓ oz.

INGREDIENTS

KEY

- ■ Cherry Brandy
- ■ Brandy
- ■ Coffee

DESCRIPTION

The Blackjack is an interesting combination of brandy and coffee. This cocktail is fitting for a game night full of poker or, of course, blackjack.

BEST OCCASION

TIME REQUIRED   **2 MINUTES**

Prep: 1 min   Mix: 1 min

PROPORTIONS

FINISHED DRINK

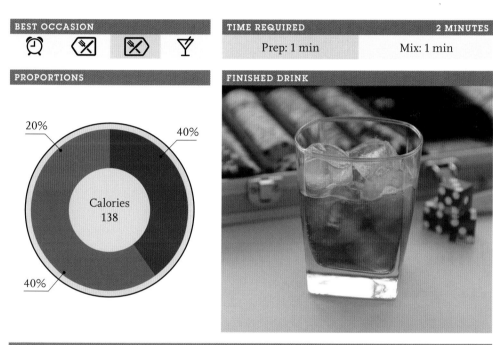

20%

40%

Calories
138

40%

INSTRUCTIONS

1 Combine cherry brandy, brandy, and coffee in a shaker. **2** Shake with ice. **3** Strain into a rocks glass with ice.

1	2	3

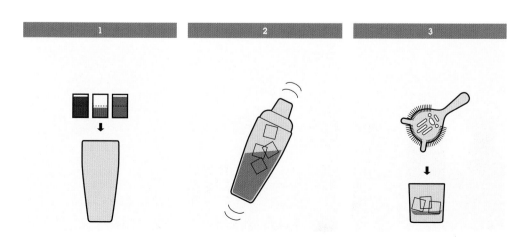

Ferrari

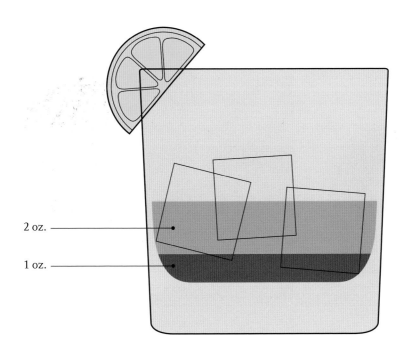

2 oz. —————

1 oz. —————

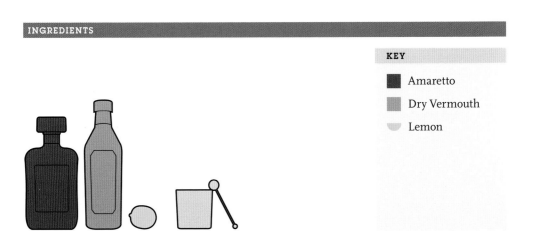

KEY

- Amaretto
- Dry Vermouth
- Lemon

DESCRIPTION

Named after the venerable Italian sports car maker, the Ferrari is an intriguing duo cocktail balanced with amaretto and dry vermouth. Test drive this at home.

BEST OCCASION

TIME REQUIRED   2½ MINUTES

Prep: 2 min   Mix: 30 sec

PROPORTIONS

FINISHED DRINK

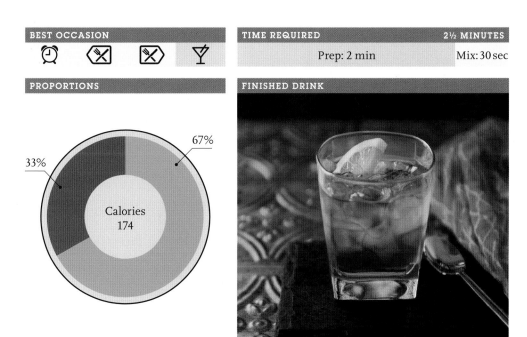

67%

33%

Calories
174

INSTRUCTIONS

1 Pour amaretto and dry vermouth into a rocks glass with ice. **2** Stir well. **3** Garnish with a lemon wedge.

| 1 | 2 | 3 |

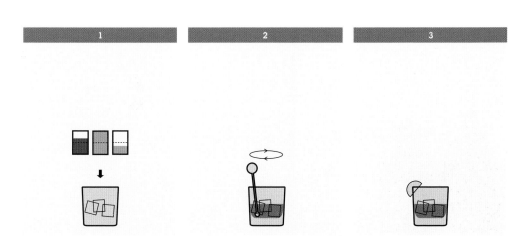

French Connection

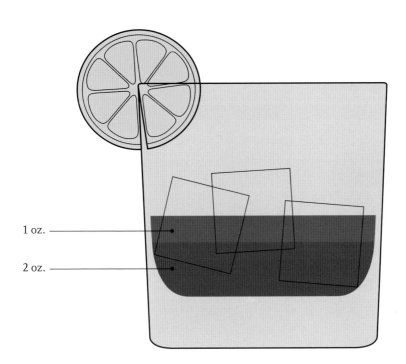

1 oz.

2 oz.

INGREDIENTS

KEY

■ Cognac

■ Amaretto

■ Lemon

DESCRIPTION

The French Connection is a classic after-dinner drink, combining the warmth of cognac with the smooth almond flavor of amaretto. This cocktail also makes for a perfect nightcap.

BEST OCCASION

TIME REQUIRED   2½ MINUTES

Prep: 2 min   Mix: 30 sec

PROPORTIONS

33%

67%

Calories
248

FINISHED DRINK

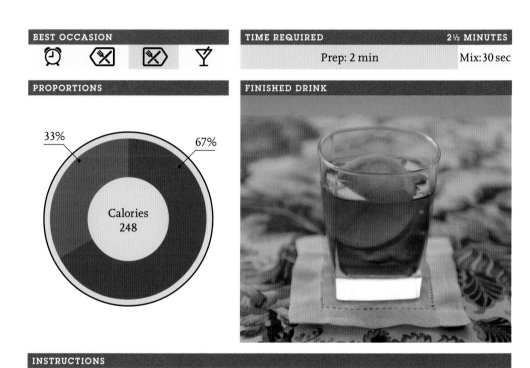

INSTRUCTIONS

1 Pour cognac and amaretto into a rocks glass with ice. **2** Garnish with a lemon wheel.

1	2

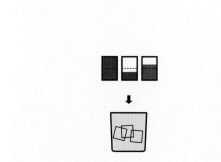

Fuzzy Navel

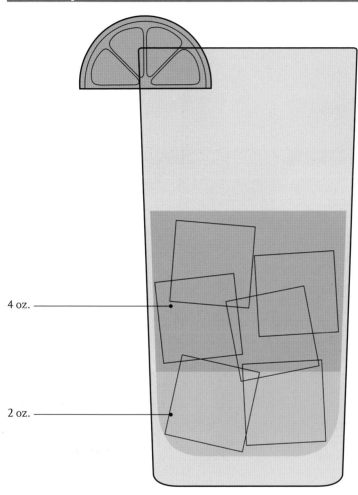

4 oz.

2 oz.

INGREDIENTS

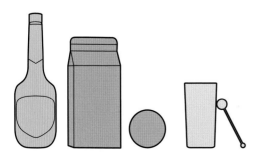

DESCRIPTION

The Fuzzy Navel is a drink that first gained popularity in the 1980s. The "fuzzy" refers to the peach flavor, while "navel" refers to the orange. If the cocktail isn't strong enough, try adding vodka, making it a Hairy Navel.

BEST OCCASION

TIME REQUIRED   2½ MINUTES

Prep: 2 min   Mix: 30 sec

PROPORTIONS

FINISHED DRINK

67%

33%

Calories
200

INSTRUCTIONS

1 Pour peach schnapps and orange juice into a highball glass with ice. **2** Stir well. **3** Garnish with an orange wedge.

1	2	3

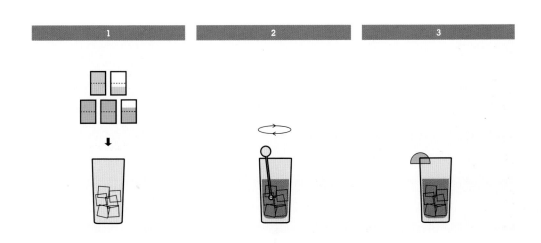

Golden Cadillac

gohl-duhn kad-il-ak

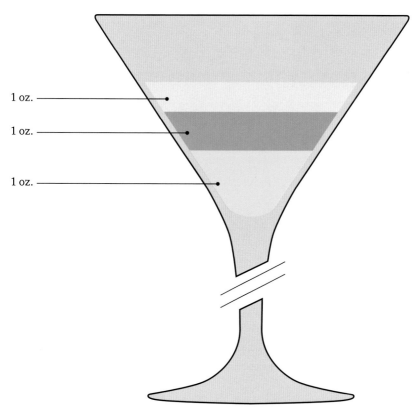

1 oz.

1 oz.

1 oz.

KEY

Galliano

White Crème de Cacao

Half-and-Half

DESCRIPTION

Introduced in the late 1960s, the Golden Cadillac is rich and creamy. The drink makes for an excellent after-dinner cocktail and pairs well with sweet desserts.

BEST OCCASION

TIME REQUIRED   2 MINUTES

Prep: 1 min   Mix: 1 min

PROPORTIONS

FINISHED DRINK

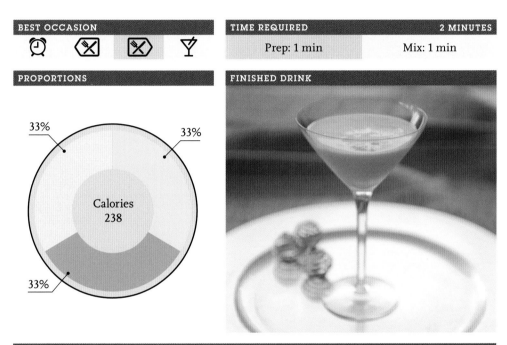

33%

33%

Calories
238

33%

INSTRUCTIONS

1 Combine Galliano, white crème de cacao, and half-and-half in a shaker. **2** Shake with ice.
3 Strain into a chilled cocktail glass.

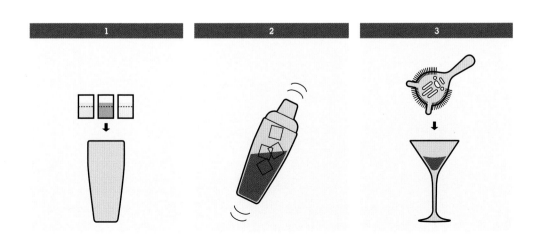

Grasshopper

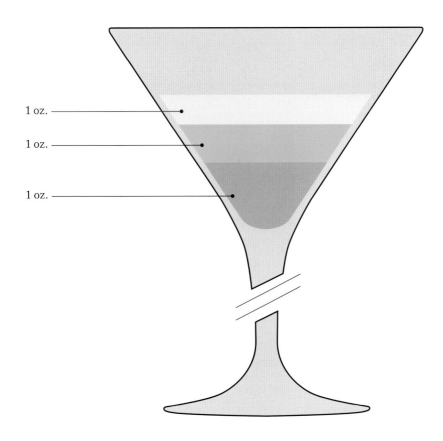

1 oz.

1 oz.

1 oz.

INGREDIENTS

KEY

White Crème de Cacao

Green Crème de Menthe

Half-and-Half

DESCRIPTION

The Grasshopper is a popular after-dinner drink. The cocktail is said to have originated in the early 1900s at Tujague's, one of the oldest restaurants in New Orleans. There is a well-known joke regarding the cocktail. A grasshopper walks into a bar. The bartender looks at him and says, "Hey, we have a drink named after you!" The grasshopper replies, "You have a drink named Bob?"

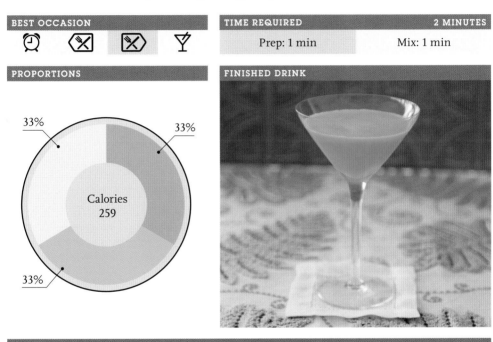

BEST OCCASION

TIME REQUIRED — 2 MINUTES

Prep: 1 min	Mix: 1 min

PROPORTIONS

33%
33%
33%

Calories
259

FINISHED DRINK

INSTRUCTIONS

1 Combine white crème de cacao, green crème de menthe, and half-and-half in a shaker.
2 Shake with ice. **3** Strain into a chilled cocktail glass.

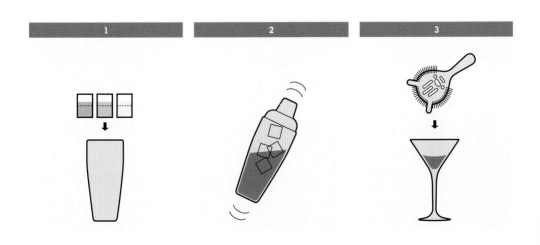

| 1 | 2 | 3 |

Toasted Almond

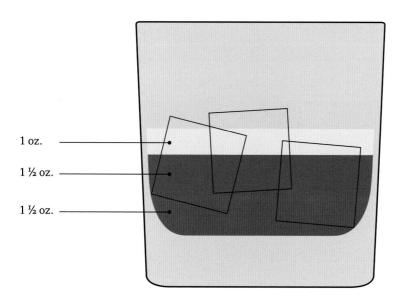

1 oz.

1 ½ oz.

1 ½ oz.

KEY

- Amaretto
- Coffee Liqueur
- Half-and-Half

DESCRIPTION

The Toasted Almond combines two great liqueurs with cream to create a pleasantly smooth and semi-sweet cocktail. Add vodka to make a Roasted Toasted Almond.

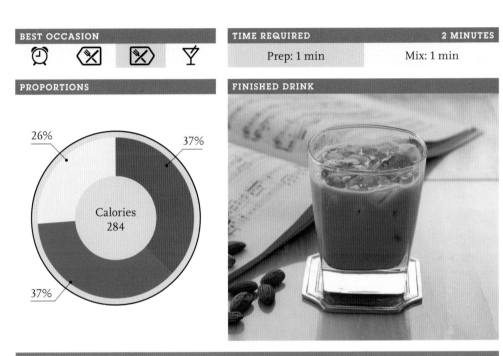

BEST OCCASION

TIME REQUIRED — 2 MINUTES

Prep: 1 min | Mix: 1 min

PROPORTIONS

26%

37%

Calories 284

37%

FINISHED DRINK

INSTRUCTIONS

1 Combine amaretto, coffee liqueur, and half-and-half in a shaker. **2** Shake with ice. **3** Strain into a rocks glass with ice.

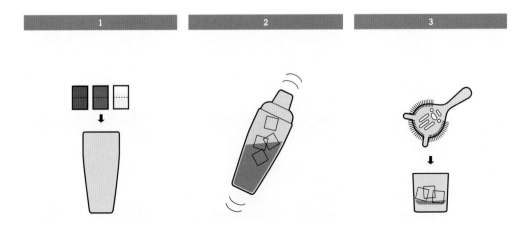

1 | 2 | 3

Index

96 Black Velvet, 38

111 Mimosa, 44

119 Bronx, 52

123 Orange Blossom, 66

127 Daiquiri, 94

133 Freddie Fudpucker, 122

133 Harvey Wallbanger, 162

138 Blackjack, 216

140 Hot Toddy, 192

145 Jack Rose, 28

147 Bellini, 36

149 Whiskey Sour, 210

150 Tequila Sunset, 132

153 Algonquin, 186

160 Kir Royale, 42

161 Gin Fizz, 58

161 Martinez, 60

161 Singapore Sling, 76

161 Tom Collins, 78

164 Metropolitan, 30

164 Sea Breeze, 178

165 Gimlet, 54

166 Cuba Libre, 92

168 Highball, 190

172 Hurricane, 100

172 Moscow Mule, 172

173 Bloody Mary, 146

173 White Russian, 182

174 Ferrari, 218

174 Greyhound, 160

174 Paloma, 128

174 Screwdriver, 176

176 Lemon Drop, 166

176 Sidecar, 32

177 Aviation, 48

178 Corpse Reviver, 22

178 Gin & Tonic, 56

178 Kamikaze, 164

180 Paradise, 68

181 Boston, 50

181 Tuxedo, 80

182 Caipirinha, 90

182 Madras, 170

184 Cape Codder, 150

186 Pink Lady, 72

187 Margarita, 124

187 Ramos Fizz, 74

189 Manhattan, 196

189 Martini, 62

189 Negroni, 64

191 Black Russian, 144

191 Rusty Nail, 204

192 Waldorf, 208

193 Brandy Daisy, 20

193 Cosmopolitan, 152

194 Acapulco, 118

195 Black Magic, 142

195 Champagne Cocktail, 40

199 Horse's Neck, 26

200 Fuzzy Navel, 222

200 Tequini, 134

202 Dark & Stormy, 96

204 New Yorker, 200

207 Sazerac, 206

208 Brandy Alexander, 18

209 Planter's Punch, 110

210 Mojito, 104

216 Bahama Mama, 86

216 Blue Lagoon, 148

216 Mai Tai, 102

217 Vesper, 82

218 Brave Bull, 120

218 Creamsicle, 154

218 Mint Julep, 198

218 Pink Gin, 70

219 French Martini, 156

220 Zombie, 114

222 Alabama Slammer, 138

228 Amaretto Sour, 214

230 Fog Cutter, 98

231 Rum Runner, 112

232 Tequila Sunrise, 130

233 Old Fashioned, 202

234 Appletini, 140

238 Golden Cadillac, 224

238 Matador, 126

248 French Connection, 220

248 Godfather, 188

248 Godmother, 158

248 Painkiller, 106

249 Between the Sheets, 16

258 Sex on the Beach, 180

259 Grasshopper, 226

272 Irish Coffee, 194

274 Blue Hawaiian, 88

284 Toasted Almond, 228

319 Eggnog, 24

321 Piña Colada, 108

327 Mudslide, 174

446 Long Island Iced Tea, 168

* Calories are estimates based upon publicly available nutrition information and have not been verified by a professional nutrition expert.

Acknowledgments

First of all, to the readers of *See Mix Drink,* thank you! I hope this book helps you become more confident in your cocktail-making abilities and more adventurous while trying new drinks with friends.

To Michael Sand, my editor at Little, Brown, thanks for seeing the potential in a more intuitive cocktail book! I greatly appreciated your feedback and support throughout the publishing process. To Melissa Caminneci, thank you for your patient help and for keeping the book on schedule. To my publicist, Carolyn O'Keefe, thank you for your tireless and incredible help promoting my book.

An enormous thank you goes to my world-class agent, Rick Broadhead. Thank you for responding to my humble email at 11:00 p.m.; our exchange started this incredible journey. I admire your passion for your authors, your thoroughness, patience, and continual counsel. I have a difficult time imagining the publishing process without you.

To my graphic designer, Will Gunderson, thank you for being willing to meet a complete stranger at Caribou Coffee to discuss a new cocktail book concept. You have a keen eye for design and an equally sharp understanding of how people process visual information.

To my incredibly talented photographer, Liz Banfield, thank you for opening up your studio for this project. You captured the "soul" of each drink. I also want to thank the studio assistants: Sarah Jane Walter, Ashley Miller, Michelle DuPuis, and Tim Olsen.

To the folks at Houlihan Lokey and McMaster-Carr, thank you for your continued support in my creative endeavors. Specifically, I'd like to thank the following incredibly smart and generous people I had the pleasure of working with: Jeff Werbalowsky, Tony Meixelsperger, Scott Richardson, Jason Price, Jeff Arnesen, Stephen Spencer, Reed Anderson, Xander Hector, Jason Vakoc, Dan Tobin, Jessica Herzig, Brian Eskew, Catie Boshoven, Whitney Murphy, and Nami Colaizy. Special thanks to fellow Irishman Ben "Chuckles" O'Connor for encouraging me after seeing the crude drawings I made that eventually became the basis for *See Mix Drink.*

Other friends and business associates who have had a profound impact on my life include: Reid and Alicia Johnston, Dan Washam, Paul Bryan, Joe and Sarah Sweetman, Jim Troutfetter, Sharon Bloodworth, Bob Klosterman, Meg Montgomery, Alison Knutson, Tess Surprenant, Mary Kosir, Paul Lotito, Zach Wilcock, Allan Hickok, Greg Tehven, Allison and Dylan Garrison, Laura and Dan Achtor, Namar Al-Ganas, Marianne Neimi, Todd Sklar, Phil Bogojevic, Mark Murphy, Ryan Tauber, Julie and John Douglass, and Nathan Denning.

I want to thank my wife, Nicole, for her love and encouragement. I also want to recognize my family for their support: Beth and Rob Carpenter, Dan and Gail Murphy, Kelli Murphy, Alex Chung, Donna Carpenter, A. J. Stewart, Stewart and Lindsay Carpenter, Bud and Marge Murphy, Vickie Udovich, Gary Peterson, Thomas and Laura VerBout, Michael VerBout, Savanna VerBout, Brianna VerBout, Emily Basinger, Francis Thevenin, Cindy Pride, Stan Pride, Bruce and Ruth Roberman, Stephanie and Eddie Ewell, and James Roberman.

Brian D. Murphy
Minneapolis, Minnesota
March 2011